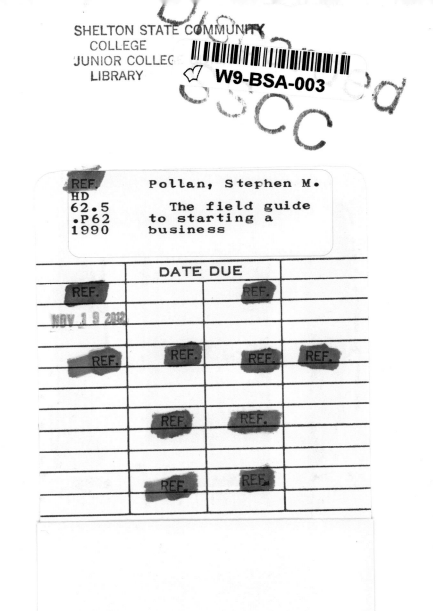

	DATE DUE		
REF.		REF.	
NOV 1 9 2012			
REF.	REF.	REF.	REF.
	REF.	REF.	
	REF.	REF.	

BY
STEPHEN M. POLLAN
AND
MARK LEVINE

A Fireside Book
Published by Simon & Schuster
New York London Toronto Sydney Tokyo Singapore

THE
FIELD
GUIDE
TO
STARTING
A
BUSINESS

Fireside
Simon & Schuster Building
Rockefeller Center
1230 Avenue of the Americas
New York, New York 10020

Copyright © 1990 by Stephen Pollan

Designed by Barbara Marks
Manufactured in the United States of America

10 9 8 7 6 5 4 3

Library of Congress Cataloging-in-Publication Data
Pollan, Stephen M.
    The field guide to starting a business.
    "A Fireside book."
    1. New business enterprises.   2. Small business
I. Levine, Mark, date–   . II. Title.
HD62.5.P62   1990   658.1'141   90-2804
ISBN 0-671-67505-2

ACKNOWLEDGMENTS

The authors would like to express gratitude to the following individuals for their creative input, editorial assistance, and research endeavors in the preparation of this book: Anthony Akel, Gary Ambrose, Charles Aug, Stewert Bauman, Dennis Buchert, Shannon Carney, Melvin Corwin, William Davidson, Dave Engleson, Eric Flamholtz, Charles Garfield, Peter Gerry, Deborah Harkins, Earl Hess, Charles Hofer, Craig Logan Jackson, David Jaffe, Jules Kaufman, Mitchell Kosoff, Alan Krasnoff, Steve Kurtz, Ruth Grad Leebron, Paul Levine, Bruce Mantia, Leigh McCullough, Ian McMillan, Valerie Merchant, Jane Morrow, Nick Morrow, Mary Mulvihill, Jacqueline Parks, Franklin Porter, Joseph Reich, Stuart Rosenblum, Holly Saunders, Erwin Shustak, Arthur Taylor, Jeffrey Walker, Irwin Warren, Kirby Warren, Peter Weir, Howard Wisnicki, and William Wulfing.

We also thank the following entrepreneurs for sharing their experiences with us: Charles Adams, Peter Aschkenasy, Caren Austin, Grace Balducci, Stacy Bogdonoff, Kevin Brynan, Ann Marie Cairns, Gene Chace, Clodagh, Christopher Devine, Tim Dobel, Joe Doria, Beverly Fetner, Ellen Fine, Marshall Friedman, Mary Gilroy, Carolyn Gottfried, Nancye Green, Jane Grossman, Susan Larkin, Joshua Lawson, Murray Lender, David Liederman, Mary Loving, Sandi Lynne, Jeffrey Madison, Doreen McCurley, Mary Ellen McElroy, Evie McKenna, Alan Miller, Randy Miller, Paul Neuman, Candace Olmstead, Randy Pike, Dana Pollan, Lori Pollan, Ivy Ross, David Sanders, Mitchell Soble, Kenneth Tillman, Ira Tommer, Nahum Waxman, Selma Weiser, Sherri Williams, Daniel Wolf, Peri Wolfman and Eli Zabar.

In addition, special notes of thanks are due to Michael Pollan for his advice and insights, and to Corky Pollan and Deirdre Levine for their continual support and encouragement.

PREFACE

Every month, some prospective entrepreneur telephones my law office and makes an appointment for a consultation. They know—either through word of mouth or from having seen my byline on a magazine article—that I do legal and financial consulting for fledgling entrepreneurs. They enter confused and disillusioned. The realities of capitalism have thrown cold water on their dreams and doused their enthusiasm and energy. They often feel there is no place for them to turn for unbiased information and opinions. Bankers, business brokers, venture capitalists, and all the other figures floating on the periphery of the entrepreneurial world have their own agendas. I don't.

I listen to them, answer their questions, and take them by the hand through the entire process of starting a business. I tell them that the only economic indicator that really matters is their bank balance. They leave my office confident and optimistic, with the foundation of knowledge necessary to be an entrepreneurial success. I am able to energize and teach fledgling entrepreneurs for two reasons: I have a great deal of experience as an attorney, banker, and venture capitalist in dealing with small business issues; and I have been, and continue to be, an entrepreneur myself.

This book is an attempt to let you, the reader, come into my office for a series of consultations. Step by step, as each chapter builds on the one before, you will slowly but surely absorb all the information you need to start and operate a business of your own. I have steered clear of the unnecessary jargon and convoluted theories of most textbooks on the subject, and have presented the facts in the same conversational style I would use if you were sitting across from my desk. In addition to drawing on my own and my clients' experiences, I have interviewed leading professors of business; the deans of entrepreneurial schools; bankers, attorneys, accountants, venture capitalists, and other professionals who advise entrepreneurs; and dozens of successful entrepreneurs themselves.

Approach this book as a department store full of advice and knowledge. The chapters in the first half of the book are the floors containing all the essentials—the facts that every entrepreneur needs to know. There may be hundreds of different businesses out there, each with its own terminology and technology, but the basic problems and principles are the same across the board. The chapters in the second half of the book are the floors containing more specialized merchandise—details that apply to specific types of businesses, specific situations, and specific types of entrepreneurs. These floors are for the individual who has already acquired a basic foundation of entrepreneurial knowledge and needs some fine tuning. You can start on the ground floor and move through the whole store, or take the elevator directly to the floor where your immediate needs can be met. However, if you do jump ahead, I'd advise you to go back to those lower floors at some point to renew your skills.

When you finish reading this book you will be able to come up with an idea that works, prepare an accurate business plan, obtain financing, get the business rolling, and bring it through break-even to profitability. You'll be a qualified chief executive, financial officer, sales manager, personnel administrator, and marketing director. You will also be a realistic business person, ever alert for the signs of danger and doom and prepared to cut your losses at the right moment. Successful entrepreneurs know when to close as well as when to open a business.

The road ahead isn't easy—many sleepless nights and twenty-hour workdays are in store for you. But the joys of entrepreneurial success are beyond description. You will be independent, both financially and emotionally; in control of your own income and destiny. No longer will you eagerly leave work at the end of the day and seek refuge from your occupation. You will find yourself working, or at least thinking, about your business all your waking hours—and when you are asleep you'll dream about it. Rather than avoiding tasks, you'll seek them out. And all the while you'll be having the time of your life.

STEPHEN M. POLLAN

CONTENTS

BOOK I

GENERAL PRINCIPLES

CHAPTER ONE

The Entrepreneurial Personality

In battle or business, whatever the game,
In law or in love, it is ever the same;
In the struggle for power, or the scramble for pelf,
Let this be your motto—Rely on yourself!
For, whether the prize be a ribbon or throne,
The victor is he who can go it alone!
—JOHN GODFREY SAXE

From nine to five—or longer—at least five days a week, most Americans toil for someone else, working hard to provide profits for their employers. And regardless of their level of success as an employee—whatever the financial rewards, prestige, or fringe benefits—most are unhappy. They long for independence; to work for themselves.

This desire for independence stretches all the way back to childhood when we stood in front of our parents' house selling lemonade. For many, the desire remains unfulfilled; a lifelong spark suppressed due to fear of failure. But that spark—the entrepreneurial spirit—need not remain buried deep within us. It can be brought forward, nurtured, and exploited to make a success of our emotional and financial lives.

While we all may desire independence, that doesn't make us all entrepreneurs. The true entrepreneur is, in fact, a rare individual. Psychologists have spent years trying to determine exactly what personality and behavioral traits individuals need to be successful entrepreneurs. They have even compiled tests that attempt to distinguish the entrepreneur from the rest of the population—one of which is found at the end of this chapter. These tests can be a good starting point, but in all my experiences with entrepreneurs—as a venture capitalist and then a banker lending funds, and as an attorney and financial advisor helping write business plans—I've found that it's not that easy to pinpoint which individuals will become successful entrepreneurs.

I began studying entrepreneurs when I was president of Royal Business Funds, a venture capital firm that specialized in providing funds to emerging companies. I saw men and women from various backgrounds, interested in starting a cornucopia of different businesses. Later, I became a banker. Many times business people came calling on me to apply for loans, quite a few soliciting funds to start a new business, buy an existing business, or expand their current business. Most recently I have been a professor of business, an attorney, and a financial advisor. In these capacities I've counseled potential and actual entrepreneurs—from designers of computer software to proprietors of aerobics studios, owners of catering halls, manufacturers of consumer products, actors and athletes—entrepreneurs all.

I've seen entrepreneurs at their best and worst. As a banker and venture capitalist I have seen them come to me dressed to the nines, with a host of information and documentation—at least the wise ones have. But as an attorney and advisor I've seen them struggling with doubts, in work clothes, trying to prepare presentations to other bankers and venture capitalists. I've met with literally hundreds of entrepreneurs over the years and have realized that no single trait stands out as the key to success. In fact, successful entrepreneurs have a mosaic of traits—some seemingly contradictory.

It isn't necessary for one individual to have all these traits to succeed. Sometimes the combination of two or more people, each bringing their own distinct personalities and skills to the business, can equal success. Partnerships can also help overcome some of the stresses—financial and emotional—that go along with entrepreneurship. (I'll discuss the dynamics of these business relationships in Chapter Fifteen: How to Pick a Partner.)

Back when I was a venture capitalist and a banker I met with literally hundreds of individuals who wanted to start their own businesses. They came in all shapes and sizes and their planned businesses ranged from acupuncture to zither repair. The only thing they had in common was that they all wanted to be entrepreneurs.

Every individual I interviewed had an idea that interested me. Their business plan enticed me into setting up a personal meeting. It showed me that their idea was pragmatic and stood a chance of success. So before I even met with them they had successfully passed the first test. Once they walked into my office, however, they quickly joined one of two camps: those who had the entrepreneurial personality, and those who didn't.

None of the true entrepreneurs had anything about them that distracted me. They were dressed conservatively. They were neat in appearance and alert. They were enthusiastic, yet sober. Nothing in their manner was extreme. They didn't look or act like the mad inventor or the artist in thrall to his or her muse. They signaled competence, intelligence, and pragmatism. The entrepreneur always presented a plan that was achievable—there were no extraordinary risks involved. They weren't big gamblers. They seemed to be well-rounded individuals.

Once we exchanged greetings the entrepreneurs got right down to business. They didn't dwell on small talk, trying to endear themselves to me. They put all their cards on the table and dealt with me honestly. Non-entrepreneurs often had a not-too-well-hidden agenda. Step one was for them to endear themselves to me. They were overly solicitous, making comments about my office or stressing how highly I was recommended. They asked questions about my personal life. Non-entrepreneurs told me about their honesty and truthfulness. Entrepreneurs didn't have to—it was self-evident.

The entrepreneurs needed no validation. They knew in their heart of hearts and in their soul of souls that their idea would work. Excitement and confidence radiated from them. All they needed from me was the fuel—money—to get it started. The non-entrepreneurs, however, would always present part of their idea and then ask me "What do you think?" They were constantly looking for validation. Rather than enthusiasm, they radiated doubt.

Entrepreneurs answered my questions honestly and intelligently. If they didn't have an answer they said so and told me they would get back to me with the information. They were really interested in having the idea work—that was even more important than getting the money from me. They had integrity. Non-entrepreneurs took every criticism as a personal affront. They defended their ideas even when they were indefensible. If they didn't have an answer they made one up. Their goal was getting money from me—not succeeding in business.

Entrepreneurs realized that this wasn't a simple business meeting between two individuals. They knew that I was judging them and their business as a unit. Non-entrepreneurs seemed to bring their idea into my office as if it were a pet on a leash. They kept it at arm's length. Entrepreneurs, on the other hand, were one with their idea. The business was in their heart, mind, and soul. They were totally possessed by it.

Whether it came from months of study or years of living with it, they and the idea were really the same thing. When I met with an entrepreneur the room was full, even though only he or she and I were in it. I could sense the presence of the business.

I can't meet with you—the reader—personally, and let you know whether you have what it takes. But I can tell you what traits make up this package called the entrepreneur.

ENTREPRENEURIAL TRAITS

No test or questionnaire can perfectly predict success. None of the standard psychological or sociological gauges—birth order, family origins, and so forth—totally correlate with success as an independent business person. That said, there are some traits that I've consistently observed in successful entrepreneurs.

• Every successful entrepreneur must be willing to work hard; not just from nine to five Monday through Friday, but twenty-four hours a day, seven days a week.

Starting Original New York Seltzer, a soft drink business in Walnut, California, required constant hard work for Alan and Randy Miller, a father-and-son team of entrepreneurs. Early in the morning the Millers were out pounding the pavement, making deliveries and soliciting new clients. During the afternoon they were at their suppliers supervising production. In the evening they were back home tabulating receipts, putting accounts in order and planning for the next day's work. "Perseverance was the key to our success," says the senior Miller. "We never let the business out of our minds—twenty-four hours a day for three years."

• That dedication and commitment requires a certain degree of good health . . . and an understanding group of family and friends.

The husband-and-wife team of Tim Dobel and Mary Ellen McElroy, entrepreneurs who launched The Tisbury Café, a restaurant on Martha's Vineyard in Massachusetts, both claim that they couldn't have done it alone. Tim works behind the scenes, while Mary Ellen deals with the public. Individually, their skills and personalities weren't sufficient for success in the high-risk restaurant business, but when coupled together they became winners. "I was life partners with Mary Ellen before we were business partners," Dobel notes. "We knew how to balance each other and how to merge our strengths and weaknesses."

• Status is meaningless to entrepreneurs. No job is too big or too small. If they have to sweep the floors they'll do it.

Lori and Dana Pollan and Caren Austin started a New York City aerobics and exercise studio. Realizing that the most effective way to get their name out to the public was publicity, the three took to the streets, in exercise garb, handing out flyers and distributing pamphlets throughout their neighborhood. After finishing their publicity blitz they would return to the studio to sweep up. "We were determined to do whatever it would take to succeed," Lori Pollan recalls.

• Entrepreneurs are supremely self-confident. They are courageous and brave. No matter how the deck is stacked against them, they believe they can win.

There are many gourmet food shops in New York City, but that didn't keep Eli Zabar from opening E.A.T. Inc. "There are two words that don't exist in my vocabulary—'no' and 'wait.' " Zabar always had trouble taking direction from others. "I thought I could do it better than the people I worked for," he recalls. "I kept getting fired from jobs. I finally realized I was the only person Eli Zabar could work for."

• But that doesn't mean entrepreneurs are gamblers. They seem to pick their spots, opting for moderately risky ventures rather than long shots.

Charles Adams received a chimney-style charcoal lighter as a gift. He found it worked very well, but the design, packaging, and marketing were poor. After discovering that the idea wasn't patented, he looked at industry trends, studied customer demographics, and figured out the cost of manufacturing, packaging, and marketing a better version of the product. Taking a proven item and developing it correctly, he and his partner Doug Fielding spawned a successful, highly profitable, Oakland, California–based business—Charcoal Companion, Inc.

- Intelligence is vital for success in business. Entrepreneurs need not be geniuses, but they must have an above-average intellect . . . and a healthy dose of common sense.

Gene Chace, a former DJ and nightclub lighting designer who opened Camouflage, a New York City men's clothing shop, denigrates his sophistication and cunning. "It really was the traditional traits—honesty, integrity, and common sense—that helped me make it. I don't know about intelligence," he jokes, adding, "if I was so intelligent I never would have done anything that required me to work this hard."

- Challenges are exciting for successful entrepreneurs. Instead of viewing them as stumbling blocks or reasons to quit, the true entrepreneur always rises to the occasion.

Marshall Friedman, an entrepreneur who inherited Friedman & Sons, his family's Denver, Colorado, paper recycling business, saw that changes in the bulk paper industry threatened to drive the eighty-year-old company out of business. His customers were beginning to develop in-house operations that would replace his own. Instead of calling it quits, the entrepreneur entered into, in effect, joint-operating agreements that benefited both parties. Simultaneously, Friedman found another niche in the market—solid waste disposal and recycling—that no one else was addressing and pursued it energetically. His ability to respond to these challenges has resulted in his business merging with another company in the industry to form U.S. Recycling Industries, the largest independent paper recycling company in North America.

- Entrepreneurs are committed to excellence in whatever they do. They care about their business. That becomes apparent to their customers and clients . . . and to potential financial backers.

Candace Olmstead and Jane Grossman were committed to making their business, The Traveller's Bookstore in New York

City, the best single source for travel books in the country. "Caring about our customers—and letting them know we care—is probably one of the major ingredients in our success," Olmstead believes.

- You won't find starry-eyed dreamers in entrepreneurial roles. Even with their self-confidence, successful entrepreneurs are realists. They may set high goals, but they are achievable ones.

Salt Lake City, Utah–based broadcasting entrepreneur Christopher Devine doesn't look to turn the bankrupt stations he buys into financial bonanzas. Instead, C. Devine Media Corporation makes them viable, profitable, and attractive to others, and sells them for their market value—a hefty premium over the bargain price he originally paid. "Rather than paying ten times cash flow for someone else's performance, we purchase at the lowest possible price, turn the station around through well-targeted programming, and then either operate it for a profit or sell it off for a large gain on our investment," Devine explains.

- Creativity is important in entrepreneurial success. In fact, the psychology of the entrepreneur is close to that of the artist. They need to create. Their business isn't a job—it's an expression of their personal vision.

Mary Gilroy, owner of Molly Bloom in Kent, Connecticut—a vintage clothing shop—sees her work as a spiritual mission; giving new life to beautiful things that have been relegated to the scrap heap or the attic. Each time she sells a garment she salvaged she sees it as a resurrection of beauty. That process happens also to make for an exceptionally profitable venture. "The business is, to me, a spiritual thing," she says.

- Entrepreneurs must have a sense of urgency. They can't be procrastinators, at least when it comes to their business. Successful entrepreneurs will get their project accomplished, as soon as they can, whatever it takes.

Ellen Fine had years of experience in the upholstery business before she made the jump into her own business—Fine

Design, a store in New York City. In order to speed up her entry into retailing, she began with a self-designed pushcart in the city's South Street Seaport area. Working on her own from the portable outlet, Fine became so successful that she could eventually open two traditional stores. She believes that regardless of how good your ideas are and how savvy a business person you are, to be a successful entrepreneur you'll have to leap into the fray. "Unless you are willing to go out there and slug it out it's not going to work."

MANAGEMENT SKILLS

To get to the finish line, most independent business people will need to start out with some management skills as well as entrepreneurial traits. Certainly these skills can be, and must be, developed along the way—as we will see in later chapters—but it greatly improves your chances of success to start out with technical competence, marketing skills, and financial acumen.

Entrepreneurs must be technically competent in the business they are about to enter. That generally means that they have some experience in the industry. Many successful entrepreneurs begin by working for another entrepreneur, learning all they can from someone else's successful, or even unsuccessful, business. Still other savvy entrepreneurs, realizing that research alone is not sufficient background in a business, and not having on-the-job experience to fall back on, get a job within their chosen industry for a short period of time. MBA degrees are not required, and in fact, may be a detriment—book knowledge cannot always be applied to the real world. And, after all, it is always possible to hire someone with an MBA; but you can never hire a true entrepreneur.

Marketing skills are also essential for entrepreneurial success. Knowing your niche in a marketplace, who your customer is, and what your advertising, merchandising, and pricing policies should be are all vital parts of both the business plan and the business itself. While much of this information can be learned, I have found that the vast majority of successful entrepreneurs have an innate marketing prowess. Venture capitalists all agree that most successful start-up business people begin as marketing geniuses and learn the rest of the management skills necessary.

Financial acumen is the third management skill entrepreneurs will need to succeed. You need not be a CPA, or even a competent bookkeeper, but you have to be able to judge and analyze expenses and costs and compare them with revenue and sales. No one will lend money to a financial incompetent, and no business will succeed if it spends more than it takes in. But here is one area where you can find help from others—a team of expert accountants and lawyers. These hired guns—if chosen correctly—can add their expertise to your own, making the package both effective and attractive to potential investors.

But simply *being* an entrepreneur won't make you a success. All these entrepreneurial character traits, and a degree of management skill, won't be enough if you can't project these traits and skills to the outside world. Many entrepreneurs don't realize they need to broadcast their abilities to the world—put themselves on display in the best possible light. In a phrase, entrepreneurs' outsides must match their insides.

This sometimes runs contrary to the entrepreneur's self-centered nature and discomfort at conforming to authority. But whether you like it or not, investors will be making judgments based on your appearance and actions. That means a certain amount of attention to cosmetic appearances is required. The stereotype of the hermit inventor in disheveled clothes may play well in Hollywood, but it won't go over in a venture capitalist's or banker's office.

Investors don't care if you are a genius or if you are a warm and wonderful person—they look at you as a tool to make money. You have to demonstrate to them that you can translate your entrepreneurial traits and management skills into a bottom-line profit. They want you to have the qualities of a bank vault—shiny, clean, dependable, and solid as rock. Stability and predictability, not flamboyance and creativity— are important. That means a clean and organized businesslike appearance, and a professional, pragmatic, confident manner. Don't overdo the self-confidence, though—a bit of modesty plays well in the investor's office.

You don't need to fit into one standard entrepreneurial mold. Different types of entrepreneurs have different mosaics of personality traits. The person who starts a business from scratch is different from the individual who buys an existing business—or inherits it—and molds it into his or her own, and also different from the business person who buys a franchise. That doesn't mean the start-up business person is any more of an entrepreneur than the individual who takes his or her parents' local operation and turns it into a national concern—they're just different types. The start-up business person is much like an artist, taking a blank canvas, visualizing the end product, and then taking steps to accomplish it. The person who buys or inherits an existing business and transforms it is like a tinkerer, taking something with a history and a track record and reshaping it. The purchaser of a franchise is an operator. He or she buys not only a business but a process, and through managerial acumen, runs it as profitably as possible.

The successful entrepreneur will eventually take on the roles of all three types of entrepreneurs at various stages in the company's growth. For example, in the early stages of a start-up the business person is an artist-entrepreneur. As the business evolves it requires some rethinking and redirection—suddenly, the artist must turn tinkerer. Finally, the business is established and growing. The entrepreneur must then delegate authority and implement a management structure—in other words, become an operator.

PERSONALITY TIME BOMBS

Even if you possess these entrepreneurial traits, that doesn't guarantee you will succeed in starting your own business. In fact, many of these characteristics, while important in launching a business, may eventually become impediments to its long-term success—time bombs waiting to destroy all your dreams.

Small businesses are unique in that they are created in their founder's image. They will reflect all those wonderful entrepreneurial traits you possess, but they will also reflect your own limitations and problems. Quite often, entrepreneurial people are unable to recognize their own shortcomings. To make your business a success you will have to come to terms with these personal liabilities and either overcome them or hire people to compensate for them. That's essential since small businesses operate without a safety net. The mistake that might be only a setback for a large business can spell disaster for a start-up company. Successful entrepreneurs will be wary of the potentially dangerous flip sides of their entrepreneurial traits.

The day in, day out hard work and concentration on the details of operating the business almost always forces the entrepreneur to take too close-up a view of things. A business myopia can set in, and long-term needs and goals can get lost in the minutiae you'll be handling.

Supreme self-confidence is a wonderful thing, as long as it doesn't keep you from seeing the reality of your situation. Almost all of the failed entrepreneurs I've come in contact with were so convinced that their idea was right and that they could make a success of it that they started the business even though they didn't have enough capital—by the standards of their own projections and business plan. I've seen fledgling entrepreneurs who even tried to fiddle with their business plans to make up for their lack of funds. No matter how confident you are, *it is essential to have enough capital.* The number-one reason that start-up businesses fail is undercapitalization.

Your willingness to do—yourself—whatever needs doing may keep you from delegating authority to others. That may be fine when the business is small, but as time goes on, and the business demands growth, you may have to loosen the reins and become more a manager than a Jack-of-all-trades. This can be a daunting challenge, one that we will look at in great detail in Chapter Ten: The Pains of Unbundling.

Keeping all these factors in mind, it is a good idea to begin your self-analysis by taking the following test, which was prepared for me by psychologists Leigh McCullough, Ph.D., research coordinator of the Beth Israel Medical Center's Brief Psychotherapy Research Project, in New York City, and Franklin A. Porter, Ph.D., himself an entrepreneur in the gourmet fast food business as president of the Washington, D.C.–

based Crepe a la Carte. Their questions attempt to capture both the entrepreneurial character and its behavioral traits. This test is based on those elements found by psychologists and management consultants to be highly correlated with successful entrepreneurship. It should help you determine whether you have the drive, spirit, and energy to realize your entrepreneurial dream.

THE ENTREPRENEURIAL PERSONALITY TEST*

1. I generally try to take charge of things when I am with people.
   a. strongly agree   c. moderately disagree
   b. moderately agree   d. strongly disagree

2. I am acutely aware of the passage of time and often press myself to complete a task.
   a. strongly agree   c. moderately disagree
   b. moderately agree   d. strongly disagree

3. I dislike taking orders from others or being told what to do.
   a. strongly agree   c. moderately disagree
   b. moderately agree   d. strongly disagree

4. I would want my employees to be content, but not at the expense of the business.
   a. strongly agree   c. moderately disagree
   b. moderately agree   d. strongly disagree

---

* Drs. McCullough and Porter wish to acknowledge the contributions of Professor Charles W. Hofer of the department of management at the University of Georgia; Richard F. Tozer, principal, Tozer & Associates, Consultants to Management, Dallas, Texas; and David Bork, author of *Family Business, Risky Business* (AMACOM). In addition, the research of David McClelland, Ph.D., and Julian Totter, Ph.D., and the Caruth Institute of Owner Managed Business at Southern Methodist University was instrumental in the preparation of this test.

5. Given reasonable odds, my efforts can successfully influence the outcome.
   a. strongly agree
   b. moderately agree
   c. moderately disagree
   d. strongly disagree

6. Things which typically unnerve most people do not ruffle me.
   a. strongly agree
   b. moderately agree
   c. moderately disagree
   d. strongly disagree

7. I seem to have a much higher energy level than most people.
   a. strongly agree
   b. moderately agree
   c. moderately disagree
   d. strongly disagree

8. I believe that there is a proper time for everything, and things can't be rushed.
   a. strongly agree
   b. moderately agree
   c. moderately disagree
   d. strongly disagree

9. I have often been in the position of directing or leading projects or groups.
   a. strongly agree
   b. moderately agree
   c. moderately disagree
   d. strongly disagree

10. When confronted with a complex task, I am generally able to pull it all together myself—and in fact enjoy doing so.
    a. strongly agree
    b. moderately agree
    c. moderately disagree
    d. strongly disagree

11. Even if I disliked doing it, I would be able to fire an employee who was not productive.
    a. strongly agree
    b. moderately agree
    c. moderately disagree
    d. strongly disagree

12. Once I've launched a venture, I find it very difficult to change my course even though the prospects of success are exceedingly dim.
    a. strongly agree
    b. moderately agree
    c. moderately disagree
    d. strongly disagree

13. I would readily leave a well-paying, high-status job to start my own business, even if it meant tightening my belt considerably for a while.
a. strongly agree   c. moderately disagree
b. moderately agree   d. strongly disagree

14. I can do just about anything I set my mind to do.
a. strongly agree   c. moderately disagree
b. moderately agree   d. strongly disagree

15. Others say I have a sharp, analytical mind.
a. strongly agree   c. moderately disagree
b. moderately agree   d. strongly disagree

16. I have worked long, hard hours for long periods of time, and I would do so again if necessary.
a. strongly agree   c. moderately disagree
b. moderately agree   d. strongly disagree

17. I have a low tolerance for frustration.
a. strongly agree   c. moderately disagree
b. moderately agree   d. strongly disagree

18. I get bored easily with routine tasks and thrive on challenges.
a. strongly agree   c. moderately disagree
b. moderately agree   d. strongly disagree

19. It is important for me to be the best in things I undertake to do.
a. strongly agree   c. moderately disagree
b. moderately agree   d. strongly disagree

20. I would choose to work with a difficult but highly competent person rather than a congenial but less competent one.
a. strongly agree   c. moderately disagree
b. moderately agree   d. strongly disagree

21. My age is
a. 20 to 28   c. 38 to 46
b. 29 to 37   d. 47 or above

22. I have had _____ of experience in the industry in which
I plan to start a business.
a. 0 years   c. 1 to 2 years
b. 1/2 to 1 year   d. more than 2 years

23. I have had the following business experience:
a. a management position in a successful firm
b. a management position in any firm
c. no management experience

24. I have missed _____ days of work due to illness over
the past three years.
a. 0 to 5   c. 11 to 15
b. 6 to 10   d. 16 or above

25. I generally need at least _____ hours of sleep to function effectively.
a. 8   c. 6
b. 7   d. 5 or less

THE ANSWERS

1. Need for power—a strong one is vital ($a = 4$, $b = 3$, $c = 2$, $d = 1$)
2. Sense of urgency—a powerful one is a prerequisite ($a = 4$, $b = 3$, $c = 2$, $d = 1$)
3. Need for power ($a = 4$, $b = 3$, $c = 2$, $d = 1$)
4. Objective approach to interpersonal relationships—entrepreneurs often have to look on people as means to an end ($a = 4$, $b = 3$, $c = 2$, $d = 1$)
5. Internal locus of control—believing you control your own destiny—a must for successful entrepreneurs ($a = 4$, $b = 3$, $c = 2$, $d = 1$)
6. Emotional stability—the more stable the better ($a = 4$, $b = 3$, $c = 2$, $d = 1$)
7. Energy level—it must be high ($a = 4$, $b = 3$, $c = 2$, $d = 1$)
8. Sense of urgency—a powerful one is needed ($a = 1$, $b = 2$, $c = 3$, $d = 4$)
9. Need for power—a strong one is vital ($a = 4$, $b = 3$, $c = 2$, $d = 1$)
10. Conceptual ability—successful entrepreneurs shine here ($a = 4$, $b = 3$, $c = 2$, $d = 1$)

11. Objective approach to interpersonal relationships—entrepreneurs often have to look on people as means to an end (a = 4, b = 3, c = 2, d = 1)
12. Realism and flexibility—entrepreneurs cannot be rigid when seeking solutions to problems (a = 1, b = 2, c = 3, d = 4)
13. Need for status—entrepreneurs are willing to forgo recognition (a = 4, b = 3, c = 2, d = 1)
14. Self-confidence—an obvious necessity (a = 4, b = 3, c = 2, d = 1)
15. Conceptual ability (a = 4, b = 3, c = 2, d = 1)
16. Energy level—it must be high (a = 4, b = 3, c = 2, d = 1)
17. Emotional stability—the more stable the better (a = 1, b = 2, c = 3, d = 4)
18. Attraction to challenge, opportunity—otherwise, why start a business of your own? (a = 4, b = 3, c = 2, d = 1)
19. Need for achievement—as opposed to status (a = 4, b = 3, c = 2, d = 1)
20. Objective approach to interpersonal relationships—entrepreneurs often have to look on people as means to an end (a = 4, b = 3, c = 2, d = 1)
21. Studies show that most successful entrepreneurs are in the 30–45 age bracket, and that the best are the 35–40 group (a = 2, b = 4, c = 3, d = 1)
22. The more business experience the better (a = 1, b = 2, c = 3, d = 4)
23. A management position in a successful company is the best experience to prepare you to succeed as an entrepreneur (a = 4, b = 3, c = 1)
24. The healthier you are the more you will be able to handle the stress and long hours that come with entrepreneurship (a = 4, b = 3, c = 2, d = 1)
25. Energy level—it must be high (a = 1, b = 2, c = 3, d = 4)

WHAT YOUR SCORE MEANS

94–100 **What are you waiting for?**
You possess most, if not all, of the key personality and behavioral traits of the entrepreneur. You have the best chance to succeed.

85–93   **A good bet**
You possess most of the characteristics of an entrepreneur. If your score on the last five questions was
23 or above, your behavioral attitudes could compensate for any personality traits you are lacking.

75–84   **Risky business**
You possess some entrepreneurial traits but probably not to the degree necessary to buck the daunting
odds and be successful. If your score on the last five
questions was 22 or below, the risk is even greater.
Remember: Entrepreneurs are not attracted to risk,
they are attracted to challenge and opportunities.
Keep working for someone else—you may be pre-
mature in your desire to be an entrepreneur.

Below   **Stay right where you are**
75   You possess an insufficient number and degree of
those personality traits and behavioral patterns common to entrepreneurs.

No matter how you scored on this test, only you can answer the question—are you an entrepreneur? Look inside
yourself for the necessary traits—the willingness to work
hard, good health, a secure self image, confidence, superior
conceptual ability, an attraction to challenges and opportunities as opposed to risks, an objective approach to interpersonal relationships, a commitment to excellence, caring,
realism and flexibility, courage, and a sense of urgency. If you
find those traits in yourself and can then couple them with
technical competence, management experience in a successful company, business skill, and financial acumen, you have
what it takes to become a successful entrepreneur.

I used to close all of my meetings with potential entrepreneurs by asking them a question. "Let's assume that I'm putting money into your business—what will you be putting in?"
If they told me that they were putting themselves on the line,
devoting their total energy to the business, making the 110
percent commitment needed to succeed, all other things being equal, I would make the investment.

Remember, lending can be a lonely business. I was sitting there in my office praying that all these investments worked out. I wanted to make sure that the business person was praying with me, and also working as hard as was humanly possible. I knew that this commitment was essential. The road ahead would be long and rough—for me as well as them.

The final ingredient necessary for entrepreneurial success is the only one that you have no influence over—the current economic environment. But as we will see in the next chapter, that really isn't a problem. The economic conditions have never been better for starting your own business.

CHAPTER TWO

Opportunities and Risks for Today's Small Business Person

The chief business of the
American people is business.
—CALVIN COOLIDGE

The economic conditions have never been better for starting your own business. In fact, the 1980s could be termed the small business decade—and the 1990s are likely to see the trend continue. More than 600,000 new businesses were started each year during this decade. That's remarkable when you consider all the negatives associated with entrepreneurship: long and irregular hours; the high risk of financial loss; the demands placed on family relationships; and the lack of benefits and perquisites that come with steady employment. Those alluring positives—independence, creativity, financial growth, job satisfaction—are so motivating that many make the jump each year.

Venture capitalists universally acknowledge that there is more money available for small businesses than ever before—especially since many investors have grown wary of the stock market. In the 1980s small business–dominated industries—such as restaurants, bars, and service businesses—grew more in employment than large business–dominated industries. Proprietorship earnings are growing at a higher rate than corporate profits and salaries. Clearly, throughout the 1980s small businesses have been growing faster, reacting more quickly, and have been economically more productive than large businesses.

Being small has advantages—particularly in dealing with customers. Small companies can offer personalized service that is caring and of the highest quality. Customers seem to prefer dealing with smaller businesses. And that goes for business customers as well as individual consumers. "Boutique" advertising agencies and other service businesses, which deal with specific industries, are offering individualized work—and they are doing remarkably well. Department stores, recognizing the allure of smallness, are splitting their shopping floors up into small, designer boutiques.

In fact, retailing, once scorned as simple shopkeeping and trading, is now seen as an attractive option for entrepreneurs large and small. Shopkeeping has become respectable. Major corporations are searching the country for retail outlets to buy. Manufacturers are opening their own retail outlets. MBAs have found they can express their creativity in retailing more than on Wall Street.

Everyone seems to want to get into retail. No wonder. Retailing has remained healthy through inflation and recession, increasing in size year after year. It offers infinite chances to express creativity, can be tremendously satisfying, and affords financial security.

I've met with and counseled hundreds of retailers and once they break even, they do well. They may not have six-figure incomes, but they are sending their kids to Ivy League colleges. They may not live in palatial estates, but they dine in the finest restaurants—and invariably pick up the tab. Recently, at the urging of some trendy friends, my wife and I took a vacation on St. Barts in the Virgin Islands. It was extraordinarily beautiful—and expensive. Whom did we meet there? Not bankers and CEOs, but retailers who had just finished their Christmas seasons.

Small service businesses are also hot today. As our economy matures, personal spending on services has soared. Today, more disposable dollars are spent on services than on durable and non-durable goods. And as discretionary income goes up, people are realizing that they can make their lives easier and more enjoyable by spending more time at play than at routine, often annoying tasks. Consumers and businesses have realized that they can leverage their time by paying others to do the tasks they don't want to do or no longer have the time for. There is also a growing market in experiences—hobbies, classes, exercise, vacations, and so forth—rather than goods. Finally, as more and more women enter the workforce the services they traditionally performed are now performed by service businesses.

Along with this trend toward services there is a complementary trend toward home businesses. Industry is thinning its ranks, laying off highly skilled white-collar workers. Many of the tasks they performed are now being taken up by consultants working out of their homes. Thanks to today's technology, every service business can be successfully operated out of the home. In the past, businesses operated out of the home were looked on as somewhat less than serious. No longer. In fact, in some areas, home businesses have taken on a certain cachet. And for good reason.

Home-based entrepreneurs need not concern themselves

with the rising costs of commercial real estate, making the business launching much easier. All the money saved through a home location can be applied to other operating costs, giving the entrepreneur even more time to break even and then head into the black. Time that would normally be spent commuting to or from the office can be devoted to the business, or to the entrepreneur's personal life. Home businesses offer a host of lifestyle advantages for the entrepreneur. For example, child-care problems, a big issue for two-income families, are less acute.

The environment for buying existing businesses is also excellent. Because of the boom in entrepreneurship and small business in the past decade there are more small businesses in general. Since entrepreneurs hate to stagnate, more small businesses are up for sale. In addition, there are more options for financing the purchase of a business than ever before. Creative avenues, including seller-assisted financing, have become the norm, rather than the exception. Money is readily available from venture capitalists and bankers—even more so than for the start-up business—since the existing business has a financial track record that can be placed in evidence. Entrepreneurs who buy an existing business find that much of the hard work has been done for them. They can hit the ground running.

I believe that every single existing business is for sale—whether or not the current owner knows it. Everyone has a price—especially entrepreneurs who struggled for success and may be willing to cash in and start again or retire. Today it isn't unusual for a sophisticated entrepreneur to approach an existing business and either ask to buy in as a partner, planning to eventually take total ownership, or ask to buy it outright.

Franchising also has come into its own in the past decade. The entrepreneur who buys a franchised business can look forward to joining an increasingly large segment of the business world—more than 10 percent of American businesses are franchises of one type or another. Franchises already account for over 30 percent of all retail sales. Many analysts predict that franchising will, in fact, become the dominant force in retailing.

Franchises are less risky ventures than either starting a new business or buying an existing business. Much of the research and work has been done by the franchisor, who will go to great lengths in helping you, the franchisee, succeed.

If the current economic conditions aren't rosy enough for you, consider that the 1990s will be even more conducive to small business success. Technology—particularly computerization and information processing and retrieval—is lowering the start-up costs associated with business and is also providing new opportunities for knowledgeable entrepreneurs. Two-income families are becoming standard today, with more and more women taking the entrepreneurial path. Governments at all levels, realizing that small businesses are the primary creators of new jobs, are enacting legislation and regulations that encourage small business growth. Under the current tax code, small business ownership is one of the few opportunities left for Americans to create wealth.

Big business, noticing these trends, is entering areas traditionally left to entrepreneurs. Recognizing the benefits of entrepreneurial behavior and the hospitable climate for it, large corporations are encouraging "intrapreneurs" to develop within their companies. But even as the big guys try to catch up, small business men and women are holding their own. In fact, they are moving into the areas that big business no longer finds profitable. Even the steel industry now has entrepreneurs cutting into the large players' market shares.

Business schools also are going with the entrepreneurial flow. Universities that used to churn out MBAs are now issuing degrees in entrepreneurship. Hundreds of schools now offer courses and programs that purport to teach the skills and techniques necessary to start your own business. And while I doubt that someone can actually be taught to be an entrepreneur, it is clear that those already possessing the spark and initiative can be given the tools and knowledge to turn their dreams into reality. After all, that's what this book is all about.

This welcoming environment may lead you to believe that there are a wealth of choices open to you—but be careful. You will succeed as an entrepreneur only if you have selected a business that meshes with your personality, knowledge, and experience. Someone who thrives on meeting new people and interacting with customers will fail if isolated in a home service business. Similarly, a loner who loves privacy and hates small talk will never make it as a retailer. And if you have no experience in a particular industry, don't think you can become instantly successful in it. In other words: Be honest about your skills and limitations, likes and dislikes.

PREDICTING FAILURE

If the economic conditions are so good, you may ask, then why do nine out of every ten new businesses fail? Failed entrepreneurs and their creditors often recite a litany of reasons for business failure: an overall business recession or depression, changes in their region's economy, high interest rates, a poor location, losses from bad debts, excessive competition, a shrinking in the value of their assets or inventory, under-capitalization, or lack of management skills. As you can imagine, business people generally blame external factors, rather than their own shortcomings. Creditors, on the other hand, usually place the onus on the business person. The truth is often somewhere in the middle.

In my experience, all business failures can be traced to one of two factors. First, not all people who start their own businesses have what it takes to be a business owner/operator/manager. Perhaps their personality, ideas, skills, and abilities weren't up to the challenge. Second, they may not have enough money. Under-capitalization is the cause of most small business failures.

After thirty-five years of studying, counseling, and advising entrepreneurs I have found that the failures were predictable—there were no "acts of God" or streaks of bad luck.

That's right: Every business failure can be predicted. By separating your own ego from the business, and taking a savvy, unbiased view of the merits of your business idea, you can see whether or not you will succeed—before you invest any of your own or your friends' and relatives' money. We will see—in later chapters—how astute entrepreneurs can judge their business every step along the way, determining under what conditions and in what situations they will succeed or fail.

I'll take you through these steps and judgments in subsequent chapters, but first I'd like to tell you about two entrepreneurs I've worked with who failed in their business ventures—one due to poor management skills, and the other due to under-capitalization.

In 1983 Nanci decided to enter the novelty-gift business. (Nanci is still so upset by her failure at business that she prefers I not use her full name.) She made her own inspirational plaques. Beautifully hand-carved, the wooden wall hangings had biblical and philosophical quotations drawn on them in calligraphy. She began the business with what she thought was a sizable nest egg and enormous energy.

At first, working out of her home, she tried to sell her wares by mail order. The advertising costs soon proved to be too high for her meager funds. The inexpensive ads she could afford were not effective.

Next, she hit on the idea of selling direct to the consumer through flea markets. Unfortunately, those shoppers weren't the right audience for her products.

After two years of this uphill battle, Nanci decided to try wholesale sales. She approached the major retail outlets that carry these products—card stores, gift shops, and religious goods sellers—but found that all the major chains were tied to large suppliers and wouldn't handle products from independent vendors.

Finally, in 1986, Nanci decided to go for broke and invest her remaining capital in a booth at a regional trade show. She had finally reached her audience, but her booth was in a terrible location and the little traffic she did attract wasn't enough to even recoup the exhibiting fees, which pushed her failing business over the brink.

After the business failed Nanci fell into a deep depression. She felt inadequate and foolish. The only emotion she could compare it to was grief. Most entrepreneurs think of their business as their child, so it is no surprise that she felt grief over its loss.

Nanci violated some of the cardinal rules of starting a business. She never really identified her customers. Without this she couldn't develop a sales and marketing plan to reach them. And without a business plan containing financial projections for both costs and revenues she couldn't budget her capital effectively. She had no goals—and she just was not an effective manager.

Josh Lawson began his taxi company with a mission—to prove the skeptics wrong. When he moved from Martha's Vineyard, Massachusetts, to Steamboat Springs, Colorado, Lawson saw an opening in the transportation business. The town had only one taxi company and he felt he could compete with them. And he did.

Starting slowly, Lawson used his meager capital to acquire a license to operate a cab company and to launch his fleet. Through excellent marketing and lots of hard work, his company grew quickly—too quickly, in fact. In his first year of operation his revenue was $80,000. The next year revenue shot up to $326,000, then $675,000 the following year. After that it jumped even further, to $750,000. New services were being added constantly.

Since the business was seasonal, Lawson expanded into other areas to even out his revenues over twelve months. All this expansion was capitalized with his growing cash flow, rather than with an influx of new financing. He thought that all the cash he took in was profit. Actually, most of it was needed to cover his ever-expanding overhead costs. He had to keep expanding to get more cash, and then kept using the added cash to expand again—a destructive spiral.

Even as his company grew dramatically, Lawson found himself in a tightening financial vise. His attempts at "bootstrapping" and all his expansion couldn't compensate for his inadequate start-up capital. He suffered a cash crisis and couldn't pull out of it. His company literally grew to death.

Lawson fell victim to the second fatal flaw in small businesses—under-capitalization. His idea was on target. His marketing and sales approach was excellent. But without the adequate start-up financing he was doomed from the start.

But even with these failures behind them, Nanci and Josh Lawson still have the urge to start their own businesses— that's how brightly the entrepreneurial spark burns within them. Both are convinced that with their newfound knowledge and experience they can make their next enterprises a success. This recurring need to strike out on their own, whether or not their ventures succeed, is a common trait among entrepreneurs. It seems you can't keep a true entrepreneur down.

And perhaps with their experience they both will go on to become successful entrepreneurs, able to predict their business's future through savvy planning. They will have to begin with a thorough analysis of their idea.

CHAPTER THREE

The Idea

Others go to bed with their mistresses;
I with my ideas.
—JOSÉ MARTÍ

Anyone capable of spelling his or her own name can come up with an idea for a successful business. Ideas are not sudden sparks of inspiration. Rather, they are logical, pragmatic concepts, which often evolve only after months of thought and study. In all the years I have worked with entrepreneurs I have never seen an idea strike someone like a bolt of lightning from the blue. God is not responsible for starting businesses—entrepreneurs are.

I firmly believe that the best way to come up with an idea for a business is to immerse yourself in study, thought, and contemplation. It is possible to lock yourself in a room and come out with a workable idea. I'm not talking about inventing the wheel. The ideas you are looking for should be achievable, relatively simple, and fail-safe. At this stage in the business's development you may not know how long it will take for the idea to work, but you should be sure that it will work eventually.

Before you can come up with a good idea, you have to be in the right state of mind. Ideas won't come if you are worried about timing, concerned about the approval of your spouse, or distressed about paying your bills. Setting criteria for ideas—such as that they have to be profitable in six months, or that they have to be achievable through part-time work— restrains your creativity. To come up with the idea you must be free of timetables and requirements. If you go into the idea-producing process without inhibitions or hangups, and you give yourself some time, you will come up with an idea that can work. All you need is the willingness to work hard. Keep in mind that failure is predictable—so you can dispense with many of those financial fears for now. At every step along the way we will be able to check your business's vital signs.

THE THREE BASIC IDEAS

The reason I am so confident of every thinking person's ability come up with a workable idea is that, after you analyze it, there are only three kinds of ideas in the world: something that addresses an existing need that has previously gone unsatisfied, something that addresses an existing need better than any of the alternatives, and something that is so revolutionary that it creates its own need. (This goes for both starting a new business and buying an existing business.) Let's look at these three fundamental ideas more closely.

One of the most common ideas used to start new businesses, or to expand existing businesses, is the introduction of a new product or service that addresses a need of the customer that has previously gone unsatisfied. This is the innovative idea. Most often, the idea arises from the entrepreneur realizing that he or she has a need that isn't being addressed and then figuring out how to satisfy it. The entrepreneur's satisfaction then is translated into customer satisfaction. The trick here is to make sure that there really is an existing need for your idea. Simply inventing something isn't enough: Someone has to be willing to buy it.

Nahum Waxman, for example, was an editor with a major book publishing company. After many years in the business he realized that there was a void in the New York City market—a need that wasn't being addressed. Even though the city was known as the food capital of the world, there was no retail bookstore that specialized in cooking. He quit his publishing job—"I knew it couldn't be done as a hobby"—and opened Kitchen Arts & Letters, which has become the nation's premier cooking bookstore.

For years, Doreen McCurley had worked for major companies—Bloomingdale's, American Express, Macmillan—starting up their mail order and catalog operations. "I would come into the company, start from scratch, and put them into the mail order business," she recalls. Discovering that there were hundreds of companies looking for someone to provide that service, she struck out on her own and launched McCurley Direct, Inc., a consulting business that addressed this need.

Daniel Wolf always loved old photographs. While in college he began collecting them. During the summer he would sell the photos on the sidewalk in front of the Metropolitan Museum of Art in New York City. He found that there wasn't a single gallery specializing in nineteenth-century photography. Wolf jumped into the gap in the market and opened Daniel Wolf, Inc.

There's nothing so wonderful as a one-of-a-kind gift. Evie

McKenna and Mitchell Soble found that out from their friends. Both McKenna and Soble knew from firsthand experience that artists often make gifts for their friends. They also knew that there was no store in New York City selling this type of gift or collectible. Using their connections with area artists, McKenna and Soble brought these objects to the public. Their store, Civilisation, has been a resounding success. Ideas that address needs don't have to be original. David Liederman was walking down a street in Berkeley, California, and spied a shop selling fresh-baked cookies for very high prices. He bought some and thought to himself that he could make better cookies and sell them for even higher prices in New York. He did. His company, David's Cookies, became a tremendous success. He realized that there was a need for fresh cookies in the New York City market as well as in Berkeley, and simply transplanted the idea. I like to call this the "copycat principle."

There is absolutely nothing wrong with taking someone else's idea and elaborating or improving on it. It is even acceptable to open next door to the original—as long as you do something that sets you apart. Do it better and charge more; or offer added services for the same price. As the adage says, "There is always room for something better." That's why many businesses are founded on an idea that improves an existing product or service in some way. This improvement can be in almost any aspect of the business—design, marketing, durability, cost, location, delivery, production, and so forth.

Selling something cheaper than the competition is one such idea. I think this is unwise, however, since it only invites the competition to follow suit. On the other hand, selling a similar product or service for more money is a great idea—especially if it doesn't cost any more to produce and it offers added value or benefit.

Murray Lender was born into the bagel business. Along with his brothers, he ran a family bagel bakery, founded in 1927, in New Haven, Connecticut. Traditionally, bagel baking was a neighborhood business. Lender, obsessed with expanding the family business and bringing an aspect of his culture to the general population, began mass producing bagels in tremendous numbers and offering them in freezer packages to supermarkets. He made buying bagels more convenient, and in doing so, dramatically expanded the customer base for the product. "I created excitement, brought attention to the product," he recalls. "I wanted to make a better bagel, and to make more of them, and faster, than anyone."

There are thousands of public relations firms in America. Mary Loving and Carolyn Gottfried had dealt with many of them in their fashion industry–related careers. It dawned on them that there was no public relations firm that specialized in addressing the needs of the fashion industry. None of the existing firms had the expertise to know the needs of both the clothing manufacturer and the fashion industry press. They had that expertise and used it to launch Gottfried and Loving Inc., Public Relations.

Ivy Ross, Sherri Williams, and the designer Clodagh had experience in (respectively) product development, retail, and design. They saw that furniture and accessory designers had to work with manufacturers in order to get their wares onto the market. In the process, art lost out to commercialism. "Why couldn't we start a retail furniture business that did product development directly with artists, helping them do their own manufacturing?" Williams asked the others. Using this non-traditional way of doing business—which allowed them to charge higher prices—the three women launched Clodagh, Ross & Williams.

Sometimes an idea is so revolutionary that it creates its own need—where none existed before. The videocassette recorder is a good example. Before it existed, most consumers couldn't come up with reasons for wanting to record television programs, and there was no mass of taped movies out there going unwatched due to lack of equipment. It was only after the product was introduced that needs for it began to develop. Today, it is hard to find a family that doesn't "need" a VCR—even though ten years ago they got along just fine without it.

This type of idea can be exceptionally profitable. But it is next to impossible for a business person/entrepreneur to achieve. To be able to *create* need requires astronomical amounts of advertising and marketing, all before any revenues come in. That makes this kind of idea the province of big business. Individuals may have come up with the concept behind the latest new consumer product, but it takes major corporate structures to take the idea and make it work. If you don't have the resources of a Sony or IBM, you'd best forget about this type of idea.

That's not to say it can't be done—look at Polaroid, for example. Edwin Land invented instant photography and turned it into a major business. But this kind of business building takes years and years. This book isn't tailored for the inventor—it is written for the entrepreneur. The inventor is idea-centered; obsessed with proving the idea's merits however long it takes. The entrepreneur is success-centered; obsessed with succeeding in business, whatever the idea is. Entrepreneurs will move from one idea to another, from one business to another, in order to be a success.

I can't stress experience strongly enough. Whichever of the three general kinds of ideas you begin with, it is absolutely essential that you have experience in the business or industry you are entering. Only with that experience will you be able to tell that a need actually exists, that it isn't being addressed, or that you can address it better than any alternative.

It is impossible to come up with an idea without some mercantile experience. This book isn't about opening a lemonade stand or about starting a new hobby. It's about starting your own profitable business. And to do that you will have to have some real, honest employment under your belt—preferably in the same industry your new business is in.

What we really gain from this work experience is commercial savvy. You have to know if people will pay for your product or service—and how much they will be willing to pay. You have to know the value of excellence.

To know all this you will have to play a little game of role reversal. All the focus groups and advisors in the world won't count for a hill of beans unless you can put yourself in your potential customer's shoes and figure out exactly what that customer needs and wants.

The most widely accepted theory of human needs was developed by Abraham H. Maslow in his book *Motivation and*

Personality. Maslow broke needs down into categories. The most powerful needs, he believed, are physiological ones—nourishment, oxygen, exercise, rest, and sex, for example. Next are needs for safety—freedom from fear and doubt. Social needs follow—friendship, love, fellowship, and a sense of belonging to a group. Then come "esteem" needs—mastery over a problem, recognition of ability—which support a person's self-image. Maslow also believed there are "self-actualization" needs, which drive people to achieve their potential. Finally, Maslow theorized that there are also aesthetic needs—the desire to be surrounded by beauty.

To help understand this theory, let's put the various types of needs into a list, starting with the most powerful and progressing to the least powerful:

• Physiological needs
• Safety needs
• Social needs
• Esteem needs
• Self-actualization needs
• Aesthetic needs

For our present purpose, this is more than an exercise in memorizing academic jargon. Entrepreneurs must examine where the need their idea satisfies fits into the human psyche.

Obviously, the higher up on the list of needs your idea falls, the stronger the customer's desire will be. Unfortunately for today's entrepreneur, most of the needs on the top of the list have been addressed for many years. A more accessible bagel or a new cookie isn't really an answer to the need for nourishment. The accessible bagel leaves us with more time to do other things—things that will help us fulfill our potential—so it addresses self-actualization needs. A new, better-tasting cookie is pleasurable, hence it addresses aesthetic needs.

Savvy entrepreneurs will concentrate on products or services that address our needs for self-actualization and aesthetic fulfillment. While these needs are the least powerful, they are also the needs that probably aren't being already addressed. That means the start-up business won't have to contend with entrenched competition.

In addition to examining the psychology of human needs and wants, entrepreneurs should look at general trends in society for help in developing ideas.

First, let's look at trends in consumer behavior. Consumers are becoming more and more affluent. Discretionary dollars are increasingly being spent on luxury items and services. Consumers also have more and more leisure time. This fact, coupled with their increased affluence, has led consumers to spend more money on recreational products and services. (For example, I now have a massage every week, go to a diet and nutrition center, and have a subscription to the New York Philharmonic.) Many consumers are using this leisure time to get involved in "do-it-yourself" activities, such as sewing and carpentry. Consumers are also becoming more concerned with their health and the environment. "Natural" and "healthy" have become fashionable labels. The suburbs are expanding. Consumers and businesses are moving further and further from the city center. This spread of population may open up new frontiers for entrepreneurs.

In Chapter Two I mentioned some business trends to consider: the new glamour of retailing, the surge in service businesses, the thinning of corporate and industrial staffs, the growth of home business, the expanding role of franchising, and the increasing trend toward buying existing businesses. All of these trends may yield excellent ideas for businesses that serve other businesses.

TESTING THE IDEA

Ideas are like plants. They need sunlight to grow. Kept in the dark they will wither and die. That's why once you have come up with the seed idea for a business it is essential to bounce it off others whose intelligence and judgment you respect. The two best ideas I ever had came from discussions with my wife. Put together your own focus group—friends, relatives, and professionals—and present them with the idea. Ask for their opinions. Contact venture capitalists and bankers—not for financing, but for their opinions. Who better to ask than individuals who receive hundreds of new business ideas a month? Explore with them potential problems or hurdles you will have to face.

Above all, be willing to accept criticism. Don't fall prey to self-delusion. That you came up with the idea doesn't mean it's perfect. And that someone else doesn't think the idea is great doesn't mean that person is stupid. Be logical, pragmatic, and open. Debate and discussion improve ideas—great ideas are never one-man or one-woman shows.

It's easy to let your idea get tangled up with your ego. Sometimes we treat criticism of our ideas as if it were criticism of ourselves. Divorce your ego from your idea during its development. Don't make an emotional investment in your idea until it is finished. Look on the idea as a piece of clay to be molded and shaped. Add to it and subtract from it. Allow it to evolve. If it doesn't work throw it out and pick up another. It should constantly be changing shape until it's perfect. Once the idea has taken final shape you can—and must—let it become part of you. But until then, treat it as separate.

That your business addresses an existing need or fits in with a societal trend doesn't mean that it will succeed. Before they make a decision to buy, consumers, whether individuals, groups, or businesses, weigh positives and negatives. What are the good things they will get from buying from you? What are the bad things? Perhaps the buying process itself is time consuming or cumbersome. Maybe there are additional costs that are not part of the purchase itself. In all your discussions probe for any negatives that could keep customers from buying your product or service.

Other entrepreneurs are another excellent source for feedback on your ideas. You can find individuals engaged in similar businesses who won't view you as competition. If you have a concept for a one-hour dry-cleaning business, take it to dry cleaners in another town. Discuss it with them. Get the business operators mentally involved in the project. If their business has been up and running for a while, they will probably have become completely process-oriented—concerned with operations rather than strategy. Your approach may even help revitalize them. Ask them what they would do differently if they could turn back the clock. Ask about their successes and failures. Offer to work in their operation part-time for no pay, in order to observe. It will be well worth it.

PROTECTING YOUR IDEA

While many of the fears involved in idea sharing are self-created and can be eliminated by divorcing your ego from the idea, some are real. Almost every entrepreneur worries that someone will steal his or her idea. Unfortunately, there are enough actual cases of idea theft to make even the most trusting and optimistic entrepreneur a bit paranoid. Fortunately, the federal government recognizes the need to protect the creator of an idea and has put in place a series of protective devices: patents, copyrights, and service marks or trademarks. Which device you use, if any, depends on what type of idea you are protecting.

A patent gives the holder the right to stop other parties from using, making, or selling the idea or product in this country for a period of time, generally seventeen years. Because of the tremendous amount of international trade in today's world there are patent processes available in most industrialized nations. But since we are obviously going to start small, let's concentrate on the domestic patent process.

The federal government will give patents on new, useful, and "un-obvious" (the actual word used in the federal regulations) machines, formulas, or processes; new, useful, and un-obvious improvements to machines, formulas, or processes; new, un-obvious ornamental designs of manufactured objects; and new varieties of asexually reproduced plants. Patents cannot be obtained for ideas, ways of doing business, inoperable devices, printed material, or improvements that are simply the result of mechanical skill.

There are two different types of patents—utility patents and design patents—each designed to protect a different type of idea. A utility patent is for new and useful machines, methods, or processes, or for previously manufactured products. These are both expensive and difficult to obtain. (If your idea would be obvious to someone having rudimentary skill in the specific technological area it cannot be patented.) These patents last for seventeen years. Design patents apply to the original appearance of a manufactured item. They are easier to obtain than utility patents but don't offer as much protection—even a slight change in the design will allow someone to copy your product legally.

In order to apply for a patent you will need the help of an attorney who specializes in the area. Names of such lawyers are available from the office of the Superintendent of Documents in Washington, D.C. Legal fees may range up to $5,000. A search for other patents that may already be in place can cost up to $400, and filing fees may run another $300. Utility patents require maintenance fees that can total $1,500. To top it all off, the process takes at least two years. That doesn't mean you have to put your business on hold. Once you have filed the necessary papers you can add the words "Patent Pending" to your product, which may serve as a deterrent to theft of the idea.

A copyright protects original creative works against copying. It generally lasts for fifty years after the death of the creator. Books, poems, songs, magazine articles, newspaper stories, paintings, sculptures, maps, and graphic designs may all be copyrighted. Unfortunately, copyrights do not protect the idea itself—only the way it is expressed. That can open the door to some creative "borrowing" of ideas by competitors.

You won't need an attorney to file for a copyright. Simply contact the Register of Copyrights at the Library of Congress for information. Fees, if any, are nominal.

Trademarks serve to register the name, logo, symbol, slogan, package, or any identifying feature of a product with the federal government. Anything that sets your product apart from others may receive a trademark. Service marks serve the same purpose but, obviously, apply to service ideas. These registering marks may only be used if you engage in a federally regulated business—such as the sale of products or services across state borders.

You'll need a patent attorney to help you get a service mark or trademark since the process may involve a complicated search of already existing marks. The legal fees should be slightly lower than those for help in obtaining patents. Along with your formal filing you will have to pay a fee of

$175 to the Patent and Trademark Office. The mark is registered for twenty years and may be renewed indefinitely.

Short of applying for federal protection, there are several things an entrepreneur can do to help protect an idea. First, as soon as you begin thinking of ideas for businesses start a daily log. Keep exhaustive notes on your thoughts and have them witnessed—by signature— by someone who is not directly involved in the development process. Once you have come up with an idea that you think will be fruitful, prepare a written description of it and have it read, signed, and dated by two people.

A copy of this description can then be sent to the Patent and Trademark Office in Washington, D.C., under what is called the Disclosure Document Program. The contents will be held in secret for two years. This procedure doesn't replace a patent, copyright, service mark, or trademark, but it does serve to provide some evidence of the date of your idea.

All of these federal programs are worthwhile and do offer some protection for the entrepreneur. Copyrights and service marks or trademarks are almost indispensable, and there is little reason not to pursue them. Patents are another story.

Not every new idea should be patented. In fact, unless your new product is in a high-tech area, I would discourage you from getting a patent. Let's face up to some facts. The patent process is long and can be expensive. Other patent holders may think your idea is so close to theirs that they'll start court actions. Meanwhile you will be preoccupied looking around for the money you'll need to get the idea off the ground. If you have developed a good product, spend your time and energy and money in marketing, advertising, and sales. Grab as big a share of the potential market as possible, as early as possible. That will be as good a deterrent to copying as any patent.

If your idea fits into one of the first two general categories of ideas—addressing an existing need that is currently unsatisfied, or addressing an existing need better than what is currently available; has passed your focus groups tests; and you have—if necessary—begun the process of protecting it; you are ready to take the next step in the process: putting together your team of professionals.

CHAPTER FOUR

Putting Together
Your Team

No man is an island, entire of itself.
—JOHN DONNE

Entrepreneurs, by their very nature, are Jacks- and Jills-of-all-trades. They like to go it alone. They believe that no one can do something as well as they can. While this supreme self-confidence helps make the entrepreneur a success, it can also spell disaster. You cannot make it in business without a team to help you.

The average American needs professionals—lawyers, accountants, architects, insurance brokers, and real estate specialists—to navigate areas in which they have no experience or expertise. Entrepreneurs have an even greater need for professionals, since they require guidance and advice to make up for their deficiencies in these areas. And they will need it as early in the process as possible.

The entrepreneur without professional help is like a person alone in a small boat. So much energy is spent rowing—propelling the boat forward—that little time can be devoted to navigating. Every once in a while the rower glances over his or her shoulder to make sure the boat isn't about to crash into a reef. That's not a very efficient, or safe, way to travel—and it's certainly no way to run a business.

Your professional team has to be an active part of the business. They will have the charts and maps you'll need to make the voyage from idea to profitability. Your professionals will be able to take the tiller and steer you away from problems. That frees you to do the rowing. You are still in command, but you've delegated some authority for the sake of efficiency and expediency.

It is hard to give up control, even if it is only over small parts of the business, especially for a naturally self-involved entrepreneur. Yet it is vital. You will have to surrender a bit of your control to achieve your goals. Don't worry—surrendering control doesn't mean you are going to be controlled by others. No one is an island, especially not the entrepreneur. It really comes down to a choice: Keep total control and fail or give up some control and succeed.

I've only recently become a team player myself. I used to think that only people in trouble reached out to others for help. When I saw people walk into a business meeting surrounded by professionals, I thought it meant they weren't intelligent enough to go it alone. Even though I'm an attorney myself, I thought every other professional was either a cobbler or a scrivener. I thought consultants were either past their prime or between jobs. When I *was* forced to meet with other professionals I treated information as a precious commodity—doling out only as much as I thought they needed and no more. I used to think everyone should be self-sufficient. Now I know better. I'm a firm believer in reaching out for professional help and keeping those helpers fully informed.

And professionals aren't the only ones I reach out to. Some of the most astute, intelligent advice on business I've ever received came from my wife, my children, and a few good friends. The average entrepreneur doesn't ask his or her family and friends for advice. Such entrepreneurs isolate themselves and their business from what are probably the best sounding boards they could have—people who truly and unconditionally love and care for them, who don't have hidden agendas, aren't paid by the hour, and can tell you exactly what they think without fear of dismissal. Don't close yourself off from those close to you. No matter how insightful you are, it's easy to concentrate on the trees and lose sight of the forest.

In an average week I speak to my accountant several times—gauging how my business and how my clients' businesses are faring. I consult with other attorneys frequently—looking to harvest some of their expertise in areas I'm not familiar with. I consult my insurance broker every two months, and I have a long list of real estate and business brokers whose judgment and skill I trust implicitly. My banker also hears from me each and every month. When necessary I have hired architects, designers, and contractors, and have placed myself, and my homes, in their capable hands. And I have used financial and marketing consultants liberally—both for myself and my clients.

What accounts for this change in my attitude toward professional help? Knowledge, experience, and maturity. Over the years I have admitted that it isn't possible for me to know everything. I can't be an expert in every aspect of business or life—despite the inflated sense of self I carried around in my early years. I have learned that you can become an expert simply by hiring experts. Each expert I have has, in fact, taught me about his or her field.

Today, when I go into a meeting, it is usually with some of my professional team. Even if they just nod approvingly as I make my presentation, their presence shows the other party that I consider the meeting important, and that I am both astute and prepared. I have taken on the expertise of my professionals and wrapped myself in it. They serve not only as a bulletproof vest, but also as an impressive cloak of authority. Having them in a meeting can be a wonderful device. Make sure, however, that you don't appear to lean too heavily on them. They should be there if needed, not as constant crutches.

Professionals help give the entrepreneur the trappings of stability and management skills—areas that investors will be looking at carefully. Mature, seasoned professionals can pass on their maturity and seasoning to their clients. And good professionals will have contacts that can help the entrepreneur each step along the way. Their contacts can become yours.

That's why it is essential that the professionals you enlist be experts. You don't want your nephew who just graduated law school to learn about corporate law on your account. Experts can trim years off your efforts to reach profitability. You—the entrepreneur—should be the only beginner on the team. True, expert professionals can be costly. Good attorneys, for example, can charge over two hundred dollars per hour. But remember: with professionals, as with most other things in America, you get what you pay for.

Your professional team can also serve as an invaluable focus group for you to bounce ideas off. Combined, they can form a think tank that can help compensate for the individualism and self-sufficiency that characterize most entrepreneurs. Often isolated from the world around them, entrepreneurs can become unaware of history, of changes in consumer behavior, and of trends in their industry. And an unaware entrepreneur—one who doesn't read the newspapers every day—can't make astute and informed judgments.

GENERAL RULES

With all this in mind it is time to look for your professionals. Before we discuss the specifics you'll look for from each professional, let's examine the general rules about putting together a professional team.

The single best way to find them is through personal recommendations from someone who is currently in a business similar to the one you are planning to enter or start. If you can't solicit recommendations from other business people, try contacting professional associations. Stress that you are looking for someone with expertise in commercial matters. Avoid professionals who advertise. The only accountants and lawyers who advertise are those who need to. Compile at least three candidates for each spot on the team.

Call each candidate on your list and schedule an interview with them. If they are hesitant, ask for a free initial consultation. If there are still objections cross that pro's name off your list. You are going to be looking for traits that can only be exhibited in person—a telephone conversation just won't do. Complaints about being too busy indicate that the pro won't have enough time to devote to your particular concerns.

Once you are at the professional's office look around. How organized is his or her office? Is it clean? Does it appear well managed? If he or she is taking phone calls during your interview, that means you don't have his or her undivided attention now, and won't have it later on when you need it. While diplomas are standard issue for professionals, look for association membership certificates and commendations—they show commitment, not just education. *Don't* be impressed by autographed presidential portraits hanging on the wall.

Ask about their ongoing education. You want pros who stay on top of the latest developments in their field; who don't just rely on their past. Question them about their experience and discuss what you will expect of them. You want them to be instantly responsive. How many similar clients do they have? How long have they been doing this type of work? Listen carefully to their responses. Are they packaged clichés or honest statements? Does the professional exhibit the communication skills you will need? In your interviews with professionals, remember that you are looking for a team member, not a friend. A winning manner can make things easier, but doesn't always indicate competence.

The key question to ask in any interview with professionals is "why?" Why do they do things a certain way? Why is their fee this amount? Why is this the standard procedure? Pros are used to answering "how" questions, not "why" questions. Prodding and probing them in this manner will elicit their true feelings and attitudes. If the professional admits to not knowing something, but will find out, don't shy away—you may have struck gold. That means they are honest. If at any time you find the professional lying to you, stand up and leave or hang up.

In fact, if there is anything about the professional you find disquieting, don't think twice—leave. You don't have to be tolerant when it comes to your professional team. There are lots of people out there looking for your business. If there is something about a particular pro that bothers you, don't try to rationalize it away, go on to someone else.

Once you have established the professional's experience and character, ask about his or her fee. Professional fees will eventually become part of your expenses and will be represented in your business plan, so it is essential that they be determined accurately. Never characterize a professional's fee as too high. Instead, ask why the fee is that amount. However, there is nothing wrong with negotiating fees with professionals. Just keep in mind that many seasoned professionals will cut back on their services when they cut their fee. Pay only by the hour, not by the job. Try to get a ceiling on the hours you'll be billed for specific tasks—and a commitment to keeping hours "lean." Ask if the professional charges for travel time. Try to pay only for the time spent en route to the job, when the pro is apt to be thinking about your situation, rather than for the round trip.

Arrange to have detailed itemized bills sent to you, weekly at first, then monthly. This will help you gauge if you are asking your professional too many questions and running up too steep a bill, and give you a chance to cut back before it is too late.

It is often possible to work out creative payment plans with your professionals. Offer to pay the professional's overhead costs immediately and delay payment of the profit portion of the fee until the business itself becomes profitable. At that time you can offer the professional an increased profit, above his or her standard fee. Most professional fees are 50 to 60 percent cost and 40 to 50 percent profit. Your professionals have to care and believe in you in order to represent you well. It isn't too much to ask that they act on this care and belief by delaying the profit portion of their fee.

Beware of professionals who offer to help you find investors. That isn't their primary job and it could indicate that they are acting more as financial brokers than professionals. When the time comes to solicit financing you will use your professionals, but as references and signs of your management skill rather than intermediaries.

Likewise, don't begin your discussions with professionals by offering them a share of your business. First, the professional may perceive this as an indication of your unwillingness or inability to pay his or her fee. Second, the search for partners is different from the search for professionals. The traits and characteristics you look for are different; not mutually exclusive, just different. The time may come when you approach your team members for financial support, but that will only be after you have developed a business and personal relationship with them. Third, entrepreneurs should not be too eager to hand over ownership shares in their business. Eventually, in your second or third tiers of financing, it may become necessary. But until then, hold onto your ownership rights.

Before you leave the professional's office ask for the names of the three most recent clients with circumstances similar to yours. Don't ask for standard references—they can be shills. Make sure you call each person. Ask them for facts, not opinions. Most people will give positive opinions when asked. Act like a reporter. Find out how long it took the professionals to accomplish certain things. Determine how easy they were to get on the phone, and how quickly they return calls.

Once you have selected the pro who is right for you, draft an engagement/disengagement letter that spells out exactly what you will want the professional to do for you and what you understand his or her fees to be. Include in this letter a mechanism to separate yourself from the professional if and when that, in your judgment, becomes necessary.

Nothing is harder for most of us than firing professionals. We often look on them as authority figures. For most of us, the idea of firing our accountant in particular is too frightening to contemplate. After all, if you are audited, the only person who can discuss how past returns were prepared is the person who prepared them. The entrepreneur who can fire a sales clerk at the drop of a hat often can't bring him- or herself to get rid of an incompetent accountant. In addition, the professional often has possession of documents vital to your business. In your agreement, describe in clear language when and how you can terminate your relationship, and indicate that you will want all relevant documents transferred to you at that time even if there is a dispute about fees.

Now, let's look at the specific traits and skills you will want from your attorney, accountant, banker, real estate broker, insurance broker, architects, designers, contractors, financial and marketing consultants, advertising professional, public relations person, and business broker-appraiser.

Don't be frightened by the number of different professionals we will be discussing. Few entrepreneurs will need to enlist the services of all these professionals right away. In the early stages of the business an accountant and attorney may be all you need. But as the business grows and develops so will your need for professional help. Keep in mind that professionals who claim to specialize in one particular industry will undoubtedly pull in high fees. Rather than industry-specific experience, look for pros who have a history of dealing with small business in general.

ATTORNEYS

The attorney you hire to represent your business interests is a completely different animal from the lawyer who put together your will or who handled the purchase or sale of your home. Your team's legal counsel must have a business orientation and have experience representing other business persons.

He or she will have to know about business structures and organizations and will need to understand tax law and its effect on you and your business. Your attorney will be called on to draft employment contracts, go over leases, study loan agreements, work on contracts with architects and designers, prepare stockholders' agreements, all in addition to advising you on the legal aspects of running your business. Your lawyer won't be dealing solely with boilerplate agreements, so he or she will have to be an excellent drafter of contracts.

All of this knowledge doesn't come from law school. I have been an attorney for more than thirty-five years and I'll readily admit that when I came out of law school I knew next to nothing. I learned, as all attorneys learn, on the job. When I first started out I didn't do well by my business clients—not for lack of trying, simply because I didn't know how to. Today I serve my business clients very well. I learned from my mistakes, as we all do. You don't want to be your lawyer's guinea pig, however.

That's why you are looking for an experienced, wise, and so, probably, older lawyer—someone who has either been in business for him- or herself or counseled business people for years. The lawyer for a start-up business really must get into the entrepreneur's head and understand the situation. He or she will have to know that you have high hopes, energy, and enthusiasm, but little capital. Your lawyer has to be very sensitive to your needs and wants. You don't need instantaneous response, but you do need to have someone who considers you very important.

All the varied fields of law that are involved in businesses can be confusing, even to an experienced attorney. But experienced attorneys will have the contacts—and the confidence—to consult other legal specialists when it comes to something they can't handle. And those contacts can also extend to selecting other professionals and experts for the team. A seasoned attorney will have dealt with hundreds of other professionals and will be able to recommend wisely.

Your attorney should be at least your equal in intellect and should have a bit of flair. Conservatism isn't necessary. Look instead for sophistication and wisdom. Don't go to a large firm that consists of individual specialists. Seek out a single attorney and rely on his or her ability to bring in specialists. The legal advisor for your business should also be able to teach you a few things. Learn as much as you can from your lawyer. If ever there is something you don't understand, ask about it. No entrepreneur can afford to become so dependent on his or her lawyer that he or she can't make a decision without first consulting them.

Make sure your lawyer charges by the hour, not the project. Get an idea of what the hours will be and see if you can settle on a ceiling. Find out if you will be charged for phone conversations. I'm not that fond of attorneys who always have their meter running. See if some of the work may be done by other attorneys, paralegals, or staff members, and what their hourly fees are. As they become more experienced attorneys charge more. You will be looking for someone in the $125 to $175 per hour range. Any more than that and the attorney is probably too costly for a start-up business.

ACCOUNTANTS

There is a big difference between a tax preparer and an accountant. The average accountant knows little beyond which number goes where on a 1040 form. (Never go to an accountant who is busy only at tax time.)

You should use Certified Public Accountants (CPAs). Not only does that mean that they have passed a strenuous exam, it also signifies that they are probably very responsible. In fact, the CPA exam tests ethics more than financial knowledge. As CPA licenses can be lost, CPAs must be as pure as freshly fallen snow. Banks and other lenders regard CPA stationery as sacred. Junior bankers and venture capitalists are trained to accept letters from CPAs as divine pronouncements. They believe that from a CPA comes truth. In fact, many third-party investors will require that your accountant be a CPA.

There have been times when a statement on a loan or mortgage application from one of my clients has been questioned by a banker. I immediately ask the banker if he or she would like to have a letter from a CPA backing up the information. Invariably, such a letter has served as ironclad proof of the validity of the information in question.

Your accountant will have to help you prepare budgets and cash flow statements for your business plan. He or she will need to be able to do projections based on sound, defensible assumptions and should know how to evaluate balance sheets and how to prepare profit and loss statements.

It's a bonus if your accountant knows about "quick" ratios, turnover ratios, and other banking terms. And any credit background that your accountant has will be a great deal of help in your dealings with potential investors and lenders.

The CPA will help you estimate your start-up costs and determine exactly what your fixed and variable costs will be—essential information in calculating your break-even point, which we will do in the next chapter. He or she will put a financial structure and organization in place. Inventory controls and dating and rating of accounts receivable will all fall to your accountant.

These internal financial structures are essential for a business to succeed. Numbers are the only way for you to take the pulse of your business—a way to predict your success or failure. I have rarely met a new entrepreneur who could do this on his or her own. The accountant will also be able to serve as a check on the honesty and integrity of your staff, showing you how to watch your cash and inventory. He or she will be your advisor on computerization as well, and should be well versed in that topic.

Nothing impressed me more than the young accountant who came into a client's business three months before the end of the fiscal year and, with his laptop computer, ran through five different ways of filing taxes—all this so that my client could adjust her business accordingly.

It's all right if your accountant sweats a lot and doesn't wear custom made three-piece suits. In fact, I prefer someone who projects stability, dependability, and integrity rather than flamboyance and charisma. But if you think the accountant looks a little sleazy, so will the venture capitalist and the banker. You are going to wear your accountant and his or her integrity on your sleeve. Your accountant should be beyond reproach. Keep in mind that investors measure you more by your accountant than by your lawyer.

When I was a venture capitalist I looked at an entrepreneur's choice of an accountant as an indication of his or her intelligence, honesty, and integrity. If I received financial projections from an accountant I respected, I knew they were well thought out and were based on valid assumptions. Watch out for CPAs who are evasive, rambling, and good with a shovel. You want a precise, responsible, perfectionist as an accountant.

Accountants learn little about the theories and practices of business or taxation in school. As with lawyers, most of their knowledge comes from hands-on experience. But, unlike attorneys' skill, the skill your accountant will need can be picked up in a few years of work at a large firm.

Look for bright newcomers—people who have just graduated from a larger firm and are starting out on their own. They should have experience working with businesses, but they don't necessarily have to know your particular industry. Young accountants are willing to grow with a client. A solid young professional will learn with you, and teach you and your bookkeeper. A large firm may make sense if you are entering a publicly regulated industry, but if you're not, opt for a small, young firm. Just make sure that your accountant doesn't have too much "baby fat." He or she has to be mature. Youthful energy is great, as long as there is clarity and common sense as well. I don't mind if my accountant doesn't know the answer to a question and says he'll have to look it up. That's better than denying his lack of knowledge in an attempt to impress me.

If your accountant has contacts with financial institutions, that's valuable—but not essential. Accountants are good money raisers, not through their banking friends, but through their other clients. Who knows more about how a company is doing financially than its accountant? If potential investors' accountants come to them with a good investment idea they are doubly impressed: first, since the accountant has a finger on the pulse of the company in question; and second, since the accountant also represents their own interests.

Your accountant should also, to a certain extent, be a good teacher. You'll want to learn as much as you can about numbers and finance from your accountant. Investors are always impressed when an entrepreneur can intelligently discuss financial ratios, profit and loss statements, balance sheets, and cash flow projections. They will look on your knowledge— which you really can only get from your accountant—as an indication of your management skills.

Accountants will charge a yearly fee that can range from $1,500 to $5,000, which covers tax preparation and a quarterly profit and loss statement. They should also train you or your bookkeeper to do a monthly analysis. Additionally, they should provide you with any other financial statements you need for loan applications or other financial purposes.

BANKERS

In the bad old days business people entered the imposing gilded lobby of a bank and *asked* to open an account or *begged* for some help and guidance. Not anymore: With a bank on every corner and the airwaves and newspapers filled with appeals from "hungry," "understanding," and "friendly" bankers, the customer has the upper hand.

The first point to keep in mind is that you are choosing a banker, not a bank. Almost all major financial institutions have identical rules and offer the same interest rates and services. You are looking for an individual who will deal with your problems personally, not hand them over to an untrained, unsophisticated teller. Your banker must be caring and concerned, as well as erudite and experienced. At this point in your business career you are not looking to the banker for loans—that will come later. Now you are concerned with having a reference, a resource. There are a host of services that a banker can offer you—wire transfer, letters of credit, contacts, cash management services.

This type of personalized banking, termed "core banking," has become all the rage. Many institutions now encourage one banker to take care of all your banking needs, from personal savings accounts and Keoghs to business checking and payroll accounts.

Forget about waiting on teller lines. You want to be treated as a valuable customer, worthy of personalized service. From this point on you can forget about automatic teller machines— all your banking business will be done with one individual. The banker for a startup business person will be called on to write letters of recommendation. The banker's name will be dropped, when necessary, as an indication of your stability. He or she will serve as your personal shepherd through the bureaucratic morass of banking transactions, keeping an eye out for your interests as well as advising you on the best ways to accomplish your goals.

How do you find a personal banker? First, ask your attorney and accountant for recommendations. Failing that, pay some attention to all those ads in the media. Disregard the numbers and rates quoted, and instead, concentrate on determining to whom the bank is aiming its advertising. Find someone who is looking for your business.

Don't shy away from foreign banks. In their campaigns to carve out a place for themselves in the crowded American market, many are using the average American depositor as their "foot in the door." As long as their money is green and has presidents' faces in the center, they are fine.

Marble lobbies and ornate buildings may give an appearance of solidity and integrity, but don't judge a bank by its façade. Small banks can be just as stable, and are probably a good deal more accommodating.

Meet with the branch manager, or if need be, go directly to the main office of the bank. The higher up the ladder your banker sits, the more impressive his or her imprimatur will be. If you are unhappy with the bankers you meet in your local area, look out of town. You are starting what may well be a lifelong relationship; a few minutes more traveling time isn't too high a price to pay for personalized service.

INSURANCE BROKERS

For too long now, Americans have filled their insurance needs through sales persons rather than professionals. With insurance costs such an overwhelming burden for the business person, a savvy entrepreneur cannot afford to make that mistake. Choose your insurance broker as you would any other professional. Don't go to a counter in a department store, or to a part-timer. Forget about insurance agents who are strictly the selling arm of a particular company's products. You want a seasoned, professional insurance broker—someone who deals with a variety of companies and who has experience in business, and preferably specific experience in your industry.

Insurance costs can help make or break a business. I'm constantly amazed by how many entrepreneurs are either over- or under-insured, in most cases because they have been dealing with an insurance person who is more comfortable selling term or whole life than business-related policies. Your neighborhood broker—the person who has handled your life, auto, and homeowner's policies for years—is probably not the person to write your business insurance.

Go to a large, business-oriented insurance brokerage firm. The insurance needs of a business are legion—worker's compensation, disability, partnership life, fire, casualty, liability, and so forth. Unfortunately, insurance isn't a licensed profession. There are no schools for brokers. The only way they learn the ins and outs of insurance is through experience. That's why you want an established, more experienced insurance broker. Your broker should be able to look at your business plan and know what types of and how much insurance you will need. He or she should be able to look at your location and determine how much theft coverage you will require. That kind of wisdom and skill develops only over time.

You'll find that a professional insurance broker can make a world of difference in your life. Large, experienced firms offer you more than just a calendar. When I was a young banker I decided to re-examine my personal insurance. I asked the bank president if he had any advice. He gave me the name of a large brokerage company in our area. I was amazed at the service they offered and shocked at how much they could save me. I also deal with a small but professional brokerage firm in Massachusetts where I have a summer home. They actually come out to my home every year and analyze whether my existing coverage is sufficient. That kind of service comes only from professional, experienced brokers.

It is important to recognize a few facts about the insurance industry.

First, no one, no matter how experienced or sagacious, knows every company and every product out there. That is why we will be checking our insurance yearly by bringing copies of our policies to other brokers and asking them to see if they can provide the same coverage for less money. No insurance company will ever tell you that it has a new, less expensive policy. It is up to you, and your broker, to find out.

Second, there are grades of insurance companies. Contrary to common perceptions, they do not all have enough cash reserves to take care of their potential liabilities. Be careful of policies from obscure companies that sound too good to be true. Insurance companies *can* go broke. I once represented a client at the closing of his company's purchase of a large factory. We had to show evidence that we had fire insurance on the building, naming the bank holding the mortgage as beneficiary. The bank turned down our policy and canceled the closing because it felt the insurance company wasn't of a high enough caliber. There is also a difference between mutual insurance companies and stock insurance companies. Generally, stock companies are more expensive, but settle claims more quickly. Mutual companies are less expensive, but are tougher to negotiate with.

Third, your insurance, as a start-up entrepreneur, is particularly important. From day one you must have adequate coverage. Financially, you are going to be out on a limb. If disaster strikes you must be adequately compensated. It is folly to scrimp on insurance coverage early on. If it comes down to choosing between drawing a salary and having adequate insurance—opt for the insurance.

How do you find this sagacious, seasoned insurance broker? Ask your lawyer, accountant, or banker for recommendations. Consult other business persons in the area. Find out who their insurance broker is. If there is a trade association in your industry, contact it and see if it has any lists of approved insurance professionals.

REAL ESTATE BROKERS

In most instances you will look for a real estate broker after you have made your judgments on location and your initial fund raising efforts. But if you are starting a retail business in an urban area, location analysis and decisions will have to come earlier, probably right after you have come up with your idea. While we will get into your relationship with the real estate broker in more detail later on, for now let's go over some general rules.

Real estate brokers really aren't part of your team, since they usually represent the seller or landlord or, at best, represent the deal itself. Nevertheless they are an important part of the launching of a business—particularly if your enterprise is location-sensitive, as retailing is. Real estate brokers are generally paid by commission; and that only comes due on the closing of the deal. That's why their primary concern is to make the deal, regardless of your best interests. Some brokers owe their primary allegiance to the landlords or sellers of property, since they choose who represents their property.

Select a broker who specializes in commercial spaces rather than residential locations. You may have had a great experience with the realtor who worked out the purchase of your home, but that same individual will be lost in the maze of commercial leasing arrangements. Your broker should also be experienced in the geographical area where you plan to open your business.

In order to test the ethics of the real estate broker you will have to ask a series of probing questions. Ask about properties the broker doesn't represent. An ethical broker will admit the good points of properties he or she doesn't represent as well as point out the negatives. Remember that brokers are not legally bound to tell you all the facts. That's why your judgment as to their honesty and integrity is so important. Discretion is essential. If at any point you believe that the broker has lied to you, or has passed on privileged information to the landlord or seller, leave and find someone else.

Better real estate brokers will be willing to work in tandem with other brokers. If they voice objections, move on to someone else. Pay close attention to the questions brokers ask you. The more detailed their probing, the more professional they are. Test the broker by providing a detailed description of the type of location you are looking for and by going out on a site visit with them. Brokers will invariably show you the property they have that best fits your needs, since it is to their benefit to close a deal quickly. If the site they show you doesn't match the requirements you have provided, the broker either wasn't listening to you, doesn't have anything to offer, or hasn't screened the property. Whatever the cause, move on to another broker. You want someone who understands your needs, has listings that apply to you, and knows enough about the business to examine all of the available properties before bringing shoppers around.

Good commercial brokers will know as much about the type of location you will need as you do—perhaps even more. If they appear to be honest and intelligent, take their advice to heart. Professional brokers will tell you that you cannot scrimp on location costs. If your business needs a certain amount of traffic to succeed, you will have to pay the price for that location. Brokers will be able to pinpoint various areas in your target location and give you the pros and cons of each.

The best ways to find commercial real estate brokers are through personal investigation and recommendations. Check the classified ads for commercial space. See which names crop up again and again. Look around for vacant sites and write down the names of the brokers representing the location. Ask your attorney to search out some reputable brokers for you, and contact your banker. He or she should have some experience with commercial leasing in your area.

ARCHITECTS, DESIGNERS, AND CONTRACTORS

Your decisions on these professionals can also wait until you have made the preliminary space decisions. If, on the other hand, you are looking for some specific type of interior that is an essential aspect of your idea—a retail location that requires a great deal of cachet, for example—you can begin to interview as soon as you have come up with your idea.

Any renovation that you may need to do to the raw site should be reflected in your negotiations with both the real estate broker and the landlord or seller. That's why the first construction professional you have to choose is a competent architect. He or she will be able to make projections and draw up plans for your changes, all the while keeping a running tally of estimated costs.

Although the choice of an architect has an aesthetic dimension, you must find someone who has had some experience in commercial spaces, preferably in your specific industry. But don't overlook the young newcomer. This is one profession in which you can afford to opt for youth. The energy and enthusiasm a newcomer brings to the project may make up for any inexperience. As with your accountant, just watch out for excessive baby fat. Look for someone who is just a little bit square. You probably want an architect who wears a plastic pocket protector. Your architect should roll up his or her sleeves and work. Flamboyance is not a plus. In fact, it can end up costing you plenty in both time and dollars. Make sure to ask for the addresses of three recent projects the architect has worked on. And make a point of visiting each one. Ask the owner if there was a cost overrun, and whose fault it was.

You have to have some rapport with your architect—since he or she will be translating your tastes and ideas into reality. The architect should provide you with sketches and designs of the initial ideas and follow these up with a model. He or she will have to prepare specifications and get involved in the bidding process.

Most architects seem to have no idea of the time value of money. They either don't realize, or don't care, that every hour they waste costs you money in lost customers and revenue. Many are immune from your urgings to proceed faster, whether or not they are paid by the hour. Often, if you want a rush job, they'll increase their fees. Try to find someone whose history isn't filled with long delays and cost overruns.

Fees and responsibilities should be spelled out in a written agreement. The standard American Institute of Architects (AIA) form is fine, as long as your attorney checks it and makes any necessary changes. Fees may be based on the hours involved or a percentage of the construction costs. Additional fees may be tacked on if you require the architect to be on site supervising your designers or contractors. If you can find an architect who is a good manager of contractors, then you've hit the jackpot. Most are, at best, ineffective managers. A call to the American Institute of Architects and conversations with your other professionals, will help get you started in your search.

Designers can kill you. They often are more obstinate in their tastes than architects, and rarely have the technical expertise required for extensive construction. They almost always charge by the hour. Unless you are looking for a specific type of design that only one particular designer can achieve, I recommend avoiding them like the plague.

Contractors will translate the architect's plans and estimates into reality, much the same way that the architect put your ideas and visions onto paper. Never use the contractor your architect recommends. You want the architect to be in a position to check up on your contractors' work, not just rubber stamp it. You can find the names of contractors from your other professionals, or by talking to local business people.

Order high-quality materials, and make sure that what you have paid for is actually being used. Either you or your architect must be on site watching the construction at all times. Keep a journal and record what time workers show up, how long they work, how long they take for lunch breaks, and when they leave.

Estimates of the cost of construction should be checked by both your architect and your attorney, and provisions should be made for when work is to be completed and possible cost overruns. It may be a good idea to offer your contractor an incentive plan. If the final bill falls under the estimate, offer to split the difference. Keep in mind that an estimate can never be considered valid without a full set of plans. In general, reconstruction and remodeling work costs twice as much per square foot as original construction work.

Try to balance the skills and experience of your architect

and general contractor—if you opt for a young architect, find a seasoned general contractor and vice versa.

FINANCIAL AND MARKETING CONSULTANTS

Consultant used to be a dirty word in America. Individuals who were retired, but couldn't let go of their interest in business, or who were in between jobs, used to, for lack of anything else to do, call themselves consultants and offer advice to anyone who would buy them lunch and pay a small fee. Times have certainly changed. Consulting is now a glamorous field. Major corporations and small businesses alike are reaching out to independent consultants for advice. The new gospel of consulting says that it is well worth the money to be able to get expert, specialized advice, without having to employ the person full-time. Entrepreneurs aren't going to be able to hire McKinsey & Company, but that doesn't mean they have to give up on consultants.

A network of independent business consultants is available today. Many are retired, but many others are offering their advice as an adjunct to their full-time employment. From academia to the corporate world, middle- and upper-level executives are offering their services to the entrepreneur.

Obviously, any consultants you hire should have extensive experience in their field, and additionally, adequate experience in your particular industry. They should have a particular expertise—financial, marketing, and so forth—and not claim to be Jacks- or Jills-of-all-trades. You have to be comfortable enough with consultants to tell the truth, and to listen to what they have to say. Prepare all your questions in advance, and before any meeting, send the consultant a package of relevant information about your business. Almost all charge by the hour, with rates ranging from $60 to $150. Consultants can start their meters when they begin to travel to your location—they are thinking about your situation en route—but should turn the meter off once they finish their conversation with you.

Some consultants do advertise, often in trade or professional journals. Others rely on word of mouth. You can find out about consultants by talking to your other professionals or contacting other business persons in your area. (Ask the head of the local college's business department for some guidance.)

ADVERTISING, PUBLIC RELATIONS, AND GRAPHICS PROFESSIONALS

As we will see later in this book, the image that you and your business present to the outside world can be crucial in its success or failure. This image involves not only advertising, but also publicity, signs, logos, stationery, business cards, and flyers—even your phone number and the message on your answering machine. For the start-up business it can be extremely expensive to hire seasoned professionals for these areas. Your budget may be limited, and therefore, you won't be considered an important client by a medium- or large-sized agency.

Look for young, up-and-coming help. In fact, try to find start-ups like yourself. A recent graduate of a design school is just as likely to come up with a dazzling logo as a major ad agency. Riveting advertisements can come from a newly formed agency—one of the many "boutique agencies" that have recently cropped up. And publicity may be done either by yourself or with the help of a young PR person.

Your decisions here are based on what type of promotional campaign you will be putting in place—we'll discuss that later on. But keep in mind that if you are putting all your eggs in one basket—if your business will depend heavily on publicity, for example—it is wise to get as much professional help as you can afford. If you will be spreading the promotional budget around, it is better to go for youth, enthusiasm—and affordability.

Finding these young, up-and-coming professionals can be difficult. If you are looking to penetrate specific media—newspapers, TV stations, magazines—with publicity, contact them directly and ask for the names of public relations people they feel are good. Call the local colleges and universities and ask to speak to teachers of commercial art; perhaps they can give you some guidance. The trick is to find someone who is willing to grow with you, much like your accountant. And the earlier on in their career you can find them, the easier it will be on your budget.

Advertising agencies are often paid by a percentage of the amount of ad space or air time they buy for the client. The more ads they place the more money they make. Public relations people generally charge by the month. PR people don't object to being tested, so if you have a particular person in mind, try that person for a three-month trial period before making any long-term commitment.

BUSINESS BROKERS AND APPRAISERS

There are many companies out there that claim to be business brokers and appraisers—acting as go-betweens for the buyers and sellers of existing businesses. But the only ones that it really makes sense to deal with are those that are run by attorneys. In fact, some attorneys and accountants function as business brokers without ever calling themselves that.

In urban areas you can generally find business brokers in the phone directory. Other good sources are trade magazines and journals. If you choose to go this route, make sure you deal with someone experienced in your particular industry. I don't encourage you to use these middlemen to do deals, but their knowledge may be valuable if you use them as consultants.

Business brokers set prices that will satisfy their needs and help make the sale. They get paid out of the cash, generally taking 10 to 15 percent of the selling price. That's very rich for my taste. Few of them are familiar with creative financing, and in fact, they actively discourage it since it cuts into their fee. The appraisals they give of existing businesses can be accurate. If possible, try to get them to agree to a one-time consultation that involves solely an estimate of value. And do that only if you are unsure of your accountant's work. The deal you get through a business broker is never as good as the one you work out for yourself.

*   *   *

The key to selecting and working with your professional team is to walk a fine line between tight supervision and delegation of authority. You want to keep on top of your professionals and guide them, but you also want to allow them the freedom to do their best for you in areas you may not be as familiar with. Just remember that they work for *you*. Never become a suppliant to your professionals. In terms of their importance to your business, they sit on a middle rung, somewhere above employees but somewhere below partners. The only individuals you as an entrepreneur *must* serve are your customers. That's our next step—determining exactly who and where your customers are.

CHAPTER FIVE

Your Customer and Your Market

*In the long run men hit only
what they aim at.*
—HENRY DAVID THOREAU

Even though your idea may serve an existing need, it's essential to figure out *now* whose need it is—exactly *who* and *where* your potential customers are. As I've pointed out, entrepreneurs tend to be self-centered. They believe that their idea is so brilliant that it is bound to sell. Wrong. For a product or service to sell, it must be targeted at both a market and a customer. And the narrower and more precise the targeting the better. Your genius alone won't be enough to make the widgets move off the shelf. There has to be someone out there ready, willing, and able to buy them. One of the first things a potential lender will do when examining your business plan is figure out if there really are customers out there, and if they will buy from you.

To be considered a customer someone must have both the desire and financial resources to purchase your product or service. In addition, the way a decision to buy is made must be studied. Buying decisions aren't always simple buy/don't buy choices.

For example: You are selling hand-made toys from your own retail store. A little boy goes to his mother and tells her that he wants one of your toys for Christmas, because his friend got one last month as a birthday present. The mother then tells the child's father to purchase it, which he does.

The father is the buyer, but is he the customer you want to target? If you are competing on price, maybe. The mother is the decision-maker, but is she the customer you want to target? If you are stressing the safety features of the toy that might be a good strategy. The friend was the influencer, so is he your customer? Not in this case. The little boy himself is both the initiator and the user. Is he your best target?

As you can see, there are no clearcut rules. Your choice of customers is based on what you perceive are the main selling features of your product or service.

Selling to consumers may be the most common direction, but that doesn't mean it's always the best route for a business to take. Reaching the individual consumer can be expensive and very difficult. But customers need not be individuals.

Organizations are the prime targets of many successful businesses. Selling to organizations differs from selling to individuals in that their purchasing patterns and buying decisions are made much more formally. There are two main types of organizations, and they have different characteristics.

Reseller companies do just that—they resell goods produced by others. Included here would be both retail and wholesale operations. The resale market is characterized by a streamlined but demanding buying process. Satisfying the customer is their job, not yours. Instead, you must satisfy the resellers' needs by providing them with products that they can sell profitably.

Government is the second major organizational market. Here the rules of the market vary widely. The Pentagon's decision-making structure is different from that of the Boise City Council. Purchasing techniques tend to fall into two main categories: open-bid buying and negotiated contracts.

It's not enough to know who your customers are or why they buy—or when and where. One of the most critical decisions you need to make is on which segment of the market to concentrate your marketing effort. The most frequent root cause of trouble is improper, or ineffective, market segmentation.

FINDING YOUR MARKET SEGMENT

Since various markets, whether individuals or organizations, have different needs, and any one business probably cannot address them all, it is important to divide your target market into even smaller groups that have some important factor in common. These groups are called market segments. For example, teenagers are one segment of the larger record-buying market. This division of a large market into smaller segments is called market segmentation. The three main ways to segment your market are through demographics, benefits, and rate of use.

Demographic segmentation separates customers by geographical, social, or economic factors. Generally, businesses are interested in taking two or three of these factors and combining them into a composite customer—young, married, and upper income, for example.

Benefit segmentation classifies customers by the reason

behind their purchasing a product or service. Some may buy furniture, for instance, because of its style, while others buy based on durability or comfort.

Rate of use segmentation breaks the market down according to how frequently someone uses the service or buys the product. This may present an opportunity for the astute business person. While frequent users may be responsible for the great majority of sales of a specific product or service, occasional users—or even non-users—could be the best place for a small business to concentrate its efforts. Frequent users are probably committed to another business. Occasional users, however, may be easy to sway to a new offering that has special benefits—benefits that you will point out to them. Non-users may include those who haven't yet been approached to buy a product or to use a service.

Segmentation will affect your choice of location, your marketing and promotional efforts, and finally, whether or not you can turn a profit. By carefully selecting a market segment and then aiming, or positioning, your product or service toward them, you can speed up your success. Start-up businesses can even break the market down into sub-segments, further pinpointing their aim. This type of market sharpshooting will help make your marketing and promotional efforts more effective.

For example: If you are entering the soft drink business and have decided to target the female teenager market sub-segment (both females and teenagers are in themselves segments), you might position your drink as the "light" alternative and stress its low calorie count. If, on the other hand, you were aiming at the eighteen- to thirty-five-year-old, athletic market segment, you might position your drink as thirst quenching—and stress how it goes down smoothly after exercise. This positioning—aimed at identifying and appealing to market segments and sub-segments—is what accounts for there being, for instance, ten brands of coffee on your supermarket shelf. Each brand positions itself a little differently, and goes after a slightly different sub-segment. The same holds true for retail and service businesses. Each woman's clothing store or advertising agency positions itself differently and targets different markets or sub-markets.

ESTIMATING SALES AND MARKET SHARE

Now that you have painted a detailed picture of your customer and the market segment you are targeting, it's time to do your most crucial research—estimating the sales you can expect to achieve by logically figuring your share of the total market. This is the part of your business plan that is most vulnerable to sniping from skeptical investors. The assumption you make on gross receipts—which is based on market share—is the one that anyone reading your business plan will attack first. That's why it has to be reasoned, intelligent, factual, and beyond reproach.

The first step is to determine the size of the industry you are about to enter, and based on that figure, the size of the market segment you are targeting. If your customers are individuals, use census data. If you are targeting organizations, pick up the Yellow Pages.

Next, look at your competitors with an eye toward determining their market share. Finding information on the market shares of players in an industry isn't easy, but it can be done. Information on public companies can be found through their financial reports, which must be filed with the Securities and Exchange Commission (SEC). The Bureau of the Census also tabulates information on some industries. There are publications, such as *Dun and Bradstreet's Key Business Ratios* and *Robert Morris Associates' Annual Statement Studies*, which provide financial information on nearly one thousand different businesses.

Once you have some idea of your competitors' market shares, you must then determine how you will stack up compared to them. For this you'll need firsthand information. This material can come through a variety of methods, including observation, interviewing, group discussions, and surveys—even test marketing, if you can afford it. Remember that other choices exist for the customer, such as not buying any product at all or purchasing another type of product entirely. Your aim here is to determine what percentage of the customer base (your market segment) is likely to buy your product.

Seeing how you stack up to the competition, and taking

into account the amount of competition out there, will lead you to a good estimation of your potential market share. If, for example, you are selling toy soldiers and market research indicates that the target customer will decide your toy soldiers are as good as the others on the market, you have an opportunity to get an equal share. If there are four companies already in the market, and you jump in as a fifth, you could project that you will pick up a 20 percent share of the market.

The final bit of early market research is to establish your estimated sales volume. Let's go back to the toy soldiers. Market research shows that nine-year-old, suburban boys are the primary customer group. Census data indicates that there are ten million such customers in the U.S. Your own studies have shown that each nine-year-old will cause two dollars to be spent each year on toy soldiers. That means the total market for toy soldiers is $20 million. Since you assume that you'll pick up a 20 percent share of the market, your estimated sales volume is $4 million.

Sounds great, doesn't it? If you stop here there appears to be no doubt that you could successfully make the jump into the toy soldier business. But before you start counting your dollars, you'll have to take into account dozens of other factors that will affect the size and success of your business. Let's take a close look at one decision that is sure to affect both your marketing and bottom line—the location of your business.

CHAPTER SIX

Selecting Your Location

This is the place!
—BRIGHAM YOUNG
(ON FIRST SEEING THE VALLEY
OF THE GREAT SALT LAKE)

For many businesses, the primary fixed cost is space, be it rent or a mortgage payment. And that's altogether appropriate—since location can be the determining factor in a business's success or failure. While there are entrepreneurs who offer some product or service so outstanding and so unusual that customers beat paths to their door, that's the exception. Don't make the mistake of assuming that since your product or service is superior it will attract buyers to an inconvenient location—it's easy to go broke underestimating the importance of convenience to the American consumer.

It's also essential that you begin with an idea and then look for an appropriate location, rather than the reverse. A client of mine once came to me with what she thought was a revelation. "Do you know that there isn't a single Chinese restaurant on City Island?" she asked. City Island is a small island community that is part of the borough of the Bronx in New York City. She was right—there were no Chinese restaurants there. But it was for a good reason—which she discovered after her business failed. The demographics of the community just didn't fit with the customer needs of a Chinese restaurant. Today, once again, there is no Chinese restaurant on City Island.

I shouldn't be too critical of my client—especially since I once fell into this trap myself. When I was president of a Small Business Investment Corporation, a very impressive group of entrepreneurs came to me with their plan for opening a music theater outside one of the retirement cities in Florida. The location they lined up seemed perfect. It was on a major road. It had terrific highway access. And the mayor of the community was willing to work with them to ease their tax burden. They showed me that Florida was a cultural wasteland. There wasn't a single music theater for thousands of miles. I jumped at the deal. You can guess the rest. I was able to pull out just in time, with losses, but also with a good deal more knowledge and insight.

The mistake of allowing a location to spawn an idea is going on all around us. Shopping center developers purchase a large parcel of land, draw up plans, and begin to scour for tenants. They show beautifully rendered plans with even the types of stores penciled in: "proposed dry cleaner," "proposed fast food restaurant," "proposed drug store," and so forth. But just building a shopping center in a particular location, with certain tenants, will not cause customers to appear from nowhere. This "test tube" retailing goes against the basic laws of supply and demand, and it can spell doom for unsuspecting entrepreneurs.

While the importance of location to a retail business is self-evident, service, wholesale, and manufacturing concerns are also dramatically affected by their siting. Real estate costs are growing faster than other costs associated with business—and can have a significant balance sheet impact for any type of company. That's why major corporations have even seen fit to create their own real estate departments.

Since the entrepreneur doesn't have a fleet of real estate specialists on staff, he or she will have to choose a location personally. The determination of location begins with a look back at your analysis of who your customers will be.

The first question you have to ask yourself is, "Does my business need public visibility?" If your business is geared to a fanciful buyer or an impulse shopper, or has to be near other businesses, a high share of your fixed costs will be real estate. There are a limited number of high-visibility locations out there—storefronts, accessible buildings, or mall spaces—so they are priced at a premium. On the other hand, if you are offering something unique, and are publicizing and promoting it, people will be willing to travel to you. Just make sure that you don't have any conveniently located competitors.

Tim Dobel and his wife and partner Mary Ellen McElroy found a premium location for The Tisbury Inn Café, a restaurant they opened in Vineyard Haven, Massachusetts. "Because of our tight financial situation I knew we had to begin making money right away," Dobel remembers. "It is possible to overcome a poor location," he notes, "by offering high-quality product and getting your message out to the public. But you also will need enough money to hang on until people find you. We didn't have that luxury."

Your typical customer already has a buying pattern or habit. He or she now travels a certain distance for your product or service, or a similar one. This range that a buyer will travel is called a trading area, and it varies depending on the business in question.

Grocery stores and dry cleaners, for example, draw from small areas. Clothing stores, on the other hand, pull customers from a larger radius, since they are a destination, not a convenience stop. Specialty retailers, such as toy stores, draw from an even larger trading area.

Manufacturers, wholesalers, and service businesses also have trading areas, though these may be an entire city or region—perhaps even the whole country. But that doesn't mean entrepreneurs starting them can be any less careful in selecting a site. In fact, studies indicate that large corporations not only spend considerable time and money deciding on location, but also are very picky, eliminating 80 percent of the possible sites right away.

Begin your location hunt with a trading area in mind, based on your market segmentation and demographic analysis.

Calculate how much space you will need, taking into account every aspect of the business that will be located in the facility. While there are general equations available from industry associations, each decision should be a custom job. I'd advise you to take more space than you think you'll need. At least then there will be some flexibility.

When Lori and Dana Pollan and Caren Austin were searching New York City for locations for their Pollan-Austin Fitness Center, they consciously looked for spaces that would offer room to expand. "We knew from the beginning that it was better to have too much space than to have too little," Lori Pollan recalls. "While it was a bit tough to carry the cost in the early days, it has worked out perfectly," she adds.

Next, decide whether buying or leasing a facility is the right course for your business. Unless you have substantial financial resources at your disposal it is wise to concentrate on leasing, rather than buying. Opt for short-term leases with extensions. A new business doesn't know where it is going or what its needs are. It can be suicidal to sink your capital into the location. The most powerful aspect of real estate is possession, and that's what a lease gives you. In fact, leasing can be very similar to ownership if the lease document is well crafted.

With all these decisions in mind, begin scouting commercial areas on your own without the help of a broker. Don't bother contacting the local Chamber of Commerce—they spend most of their time obscuring, not illuminating or correcting problems. Even the people who live, work, or do business in the area aren't good sources of information. They aren't likely to speak ill of their own neighborhood, whatever the facts. At this point we aren't looking for specific sites, just trying to get a feel for the character of the areas.

Take a look at how well the property in the area is being cared for. Are the building exteriors clean and well maintained? Are the road and sidewalk clean or covered with litter? Are there sufficient street lights—and are they all in working order? Are there many other new businesses? If so, what type are they? What types of cars are in the parking lots? Do the existing businesses seem prosperous? Are there many vacancies? Examine the hours of the stores in the area. The longer they are open, the healthier the economy of the neighborhood. Businesses that close for lunch aren't doing well. Check the shopping centers. If they are empty on Thursdays after five o'clock then there is trouble.

Try to find out whether the neighborhood is changing—and how. If, for example, a luncheonette has just closed and is being replaced by a gourmet food shop, then there is probably an upward demographic trend. The reverse may spell a decline in the economic level. Areas that are moving up tend to continue to move up. Areas that are level, or dropping in value and character, tend to continue on that course. Abrupt shifts in real estate trends are the exception.

Using the tips I offered in Chapter Four: Putting Together Your Team, enlist the aid of one or two commercial real estate brokers who work in the target area you have been scouting. Tell them exactly what you are looking for and explain what type of business you are going to open. Let them take you around town in their cars. Take notes on everything you see. Try to limit the number of sites you see each day—otherwise you will begin confusing them. Bring an instant camera and a tape measure with you on your visits to help record details.

In addition, when siting any business, study the licensing and zoning ordinances of the area, insuring that you won't raise the ire of local officials or neighbors.

Don't jump at an inexpensive location without first calculating whether it will provide you with the traffic needed to keep the business operating. And the only way to gauge traffic is to take several different days and times to stand there yourself to count passersby. Never take the word of the landlord or a broker. An expensive, high-traffic location can be a heavy load to carry, but a less-trafficked spot may mean that your advertising costs will soar. Likewise, an out-of-the-way manufacturing facility may save dollars at first, but when it comes time to transport your product you could end up spending more than if you had chosen a more expensive but also more convenient location. If a location is cheap, it's for a reason.

Molly Bloom, Mary Gilroy's vintage clothing store in Kent, Connecticut, was originally located in an inexpensive but out-of-the-way location. "I was drawing customers from a wide area, but there just wasn't enough walk-in traffic," she remembers. When a larger but more expensive location in the center of town became available, Gilroy jumped at it. "The increased space has let me transform my display from an ineffective jumble into a beautiful presentation. That, and the increased traffic, has really made a difference. The added sales have more than made up for the higher rent."

While these general factors are true for every type of business, there are some specific guidelines that should also be considered depending on what business you are entering.

RETAIL LOCATIONS

Location is the primary concern for a retail business, since its identity really is its storefront. You won't have a business to sell unless you have an assignable lease with extensions. There is no such thing as selling goodwill in a retail business unless it stays in the same location. Would you buy a retail business if it only had a two-year lease? Of course not. So don't expect someone else to buy it.

The first choice a retailer makes is whether to locate in a freestanding building or in a shopping center.

Stand-alone buildings do offer greater access and visibility, but if the product sold is an impulse item rather than a necessity, they may not offer enough traffic. This must be factored against their added space and lower lease rates. Stand-alone buildings offer control over the immediate environment and allow for expansion, perhaps even letting the retailer create his or her own little shopping center. But it is important to remember that traffic won't be as high.

Small shopping centers are strictly convenience locations. Shoppers here are interested in fast service. Developers and landlords of small shopping centers are often amenable to small businesses, and may not charge exorbitant rents.

Community shopping centers expand their focus to include some impulse-buying stores since the balance of stores in these shopping centers draw customers who are willing to spend more time shopping. Unfortunately, community shopping centers can be very expensive, and developer/landlords may hesitate to take in a "fledgling" business.

Large shopping centers draw regionally, rather than just locally. Shoppers here stay for an extended period of time, often having driven some distance. Convenience shops may or may not fit in, depending on whether their main concern is traffic or accessibility. The big drawback to large shopping centers is their rent, which can put them out of the small business person's league.

Locating in any shopping center means giving up some control. Many centers require businesses to pay maintenance fees, subscribe to joint advertising programs, or keep common business hours, all of which have to be factored into the decision-making process.

Whether you will be located in your own building or in a shopping center, your neighboring stores can have a tremendous effect on your success or failure. Make sure that the other stores complement your business. For example, a handbag shop may do well when located near a women's clothing store, but not fare well when next to a hardware store.

Calculate how much competition you will have in your

trading area. Some businesses do well when surrounded by other, similar stores—shoe stores and restaurants, for example. Others—such as bookstores and card shops—fare better when the competition isn't close by. Try to have a covenant written into your lease that prevents the landlord from leasing to a competitor.

Step back from the site and gauge its visibility. Even if thousands pass by each day, if they can't see your store they won't come in. Find out if you have the right to put up signs or banners on various parts of the landlord's building. That option could help turn a slightly offbeat location with poor visibility into a prime retail site. And while you are at it, check any regulations or zoning laws that could affect signs. Some localities restrict the size of signs and won't allow them to be illuminated. Try parking your car nearby. If there isn't enough parking, or if it isn't nearby, you'll lose drive-up business.

The last step in selecting a retail site is an examination of the demographic patterns of the area. While a trading area may be able to support a bargain outlet today, looming gentrification may mean that merchants will have to be upscale to survive in the future. Make sure that the area's demographics are stable enough to support your business for the foreseeable future.

There are also a few pragmatic real estate facts that you should keep in mind when searching for a retail location:

- A main road location isn't worth a premium price if it has a center mall or median, which, in effect, turns it into two one-way streets.
- You can be located on too big a road. If the vehicles move so fast as to make slowing down, turning, or parking dangerous, then all the added traffic won't mean a thing—your customers won't be able to stop.
- Corner locations are worth the premium they command. They draw traffic from both cross streets, often doubling the walk-in trade of a business.
- Locations near public transportation are valuable. If you are in a major urban area, sites near railroad, subway, and bus stops can mean a tremendous boost in traffic.

- Sometimes there is an advantage to being located in a "district" where similar businesses abound—a street lined with dozens of antique stores, for example. Consumers will travel a considerable distance to an area if they know they can shop a number of retail stores looking for the same item. In addition, customers in such districts are ready to buy—they don't need to be convinced.
- There are sunny and shady sides of streets. In the winter there will be more foot traffic on the sunny side of the street, and in the summer it will be the opposite. That could make a big difference if your business is seasonal.

SERVICE LOCATIONS

While service businesses must make many of the same judgments about location that retailers make, the selection of a site for a service business can be simplified if the entrepreneur asks him- or herself two questions: How is business carried out, and how does the customer choose the business?

Any business that goes to its customers—such as a window cleaner or an exterminator—can select a site based on travel time, not customer traffic, accessibility, or visibility. Conversely, any business to which customers come—such as a photo lab or a dry cleaner—must locate in a site with sufficient traffic, access, and visibility.

Service businesses used to try to locate in areas that had a certain cachet. In New York City, for example, financial companies used to try to be on Wall Street, while advertising agencies wanted locations on Madison Avenue. That no longer holds true. Consumers are more aware of the costs associated with such premium space, and may even feel that fees are inflated to help cover this cost.

If you are opening a consulting business consider working out of your home. A business can be run just as professionally from your study as from a suite in an expensive office building. If you don't have the facilities to have clients come to your home, try meeting them at a health or social club. The membership fee will almost certainly be less than office rent. Similarly, try arranging a regular table at a quiet restaurant for lunch meetings.

MANUFACTURING LOCATIONS

The prime considerations for manufacturers are that they get as much space for their money as possible, that there is a constant labor supply, that the local government offers tax benefits, that there is access to transportation and shipping, that utility costs are not exorbitant, and that zoning regulations can be complied with.

The community a manufacturer locates in must have a supply of labor that matches the company's needs. If goods must be transported any distance, there must be highway, railroad, dock, or airline facilities nearby. A manufacturer, like any other business, must have access to adequate community services such as utilities, fire and police protection, and sanitation or waste disposal. Specific sites for manufacturing facilities must be of sufficient size, have adequate drainage, and be physically able to support a large structure.

While it is attractive to build your own manufacturing facility, the purchase of an existing building may help defray many costs associated with new construction, especially for a start-up business. You can assume that an existing building already has utility hookups, water and waste systems, and road access, while a new structure will have none. The time required to construct a building may be reason enough to avoid development. There are bargains available for manufacturers. In the "rust belt"—the once-thriving, now depressed Northeastern industrial states—there are many facilities standing vacant, just waiting for someone to come along—just watch out for environmental problems.

As with retail and service businesses, the character of the community and its future must be taken into account. Will there be a supply of labor in the future? Does it appear that the community is about to upgrade its zoning? Is the local government supportive of manufacturing, or will they place regulatory obstacles in your path?

Government policy can, in fact, be a major factor in selecting a location for any type of business. Governments of economically depressed areas are often willing to help finance new business, provide tax breaks, recruit labor, even help with site costs.

A small town in Utah offered an electronics client of mine a new fifty-thousand-square-foot warehouse for an eighty-cent-per-square-foot rental, a plentiful labor supply, and they even threw in a sign. But don't let municipal incentives outweigh the other factors in judging a location. My client did. The business eventually failed because the inexpensive, beautiful facility was too far away from rail transportation. Worse still, while labor was plentiful and inexpensive, it was inexperienced and not easily trainable.

WHOLESALE LOCATIONS

Competition and transportation are the major determining factors for wholesalers searching for a location.

While certain metropolitan areas often serve as centers for particular products, wholesalers may find that locating in virgin territory can help their business. Merchants outside the product center must do their buying long distance and wait for delivery. A local wholesaler may be able to capitalize on speed and service. If speed and service aren't important factors in the industry you are entering, then locating in the industry hub may offer advantages: transportation, access, and labor are readily available since others are already drawing on those resources, and local government and utilities already have experience meeting the needs of the industry.

After selecting a region, wholesalers may choose to locate in urban, suburban, or rural areas. Urban locations offer easy access to customers and ready transportation, but can be extremely expensive. Rural locations may be cheap, but may not offer the access or services necessary. Suburban locales are a compromise choice, but can present zoning, labor, and regulatory difficulties, since most are middle income and residential in character.

The wholesaling facility itself demands easy access to transportation, since shipment of goods is the primary mission of the business. Other aspects of the site, such as appearance, depend on whether customers will be coming to the site to buy, or will be making that decision off site. If your customers are coming to your location it will pay to have an effective selling area and certain amenities. A good address, on the other hand, could actually be a detriment to whole-salers—customers may think that space costs are being passed on to them.

Location selection is a frightening task, second only to securing financing in its "fear factor." One way to cut the job down into manageable pieces is to draw up a description of your dream location. List every factor from cost to traffic to size. Be specific in your needs. Take this description with you when shopping for a location. While you may never find this utopia for your business, the description of your ideal location can serve as a template against which to measure each potential site.

Years ago there used to be industry standards for how much rent a business person should pay—usually a percentage of anticipated gross. Today those rules no longer apply. In major urban areas, and in many suburban areas, rent has skyrocketed, requiring a larger and larger share of the business person's budget. That means that many entrepreneurs will have to work backward, finding out what their rent cost will be, and then calculating if they can run their business at a profit. If your plan calls for real estate to take up only a small percentage of your budget, and you discover that's impossible, go back and update your plan.

Once you find a suitable location, it's time to bring your lawyer into the picture to help negotiate the lease.

NEGOTIATING THE COMMERCIAL LEASE

Your attorney should be called on to look at and negotiate any commercial lease you are about to sign. Regardless of what they may tell you, real estate brokers are probably working for the landlord. They may seem friendly, but they are actually out to get as much blood from you as they can. The best you can hope for is that the broker will represent the deal, not just the landlord. In any case, you need your attorney to get involved and be your advocate. While he or she will be doing most of the work, it is worthwhile for entrepreneurs to have an idea of what to look out for in a commercial lease.

Be careful to get a lease that has renewal options that extend at least as far as your anticipated break-even point.

Get a short lease with many options to renew. That way you'll get the best of both worlds. You'll be able to leave if necessary or stay in place for an extended period of time. No one will lend money to a business that won't be in place long enough to make a serious go at success. In addition, lenders will want to see that your lease extends at least as long as their loan. A business lease has to be long enough for the entrepreneur to establish customer loyalty.

If your business is incorporated, business leases should always be signed by your corporation, not an individual. Even though you are sure that your business will succeed, you should insulate yourself from any personal liability if it fails. (The question of liability is discussed in more detail in Chapter Thirteen: Choosing a Business Structure.) If it is impossible to avoid some personal guarantee, try to get a short-term lease with extensions at fixed prices.

Never believe that the landlord is your friend. He or she is a business person, just as you are. Don't take anything the landlord says at face value. At best, landlords live up to their agreements. At worst they are vampires ready to suck the life out of your business. When landlords find out that a commercial tenant is doing well they often instinctively try to share in the success by raising the rent or passing on more costs.

My father-in-law was a commercial landlord in the suburbs of New York City. He would go into his tenants' stores to see how they were doing. He really cared about them—their success was his. If the shop floor was dirty, he'd offer to sweep it. If business wasn't that good, he'd let them slide for a month or two on rent. He might even help them out by buying, at list price, merchandise he didn't really need and then distributing it to his grandchildren. He was really a professional, caring landlord. But that's an extinct breed. Today, for most landlords, commercial real estate is strictly an investment.

Make sure that your lease accurately reflects the square footage of your space. Often, landlords will try to obscure the size of the space, charging for the space under, or even outside, the walls. You should be charged only for "carpetable" space.

Examine the "pass-alongs" carefully. These are the charges landlords assess for such things as lobby areas, air-conditioning, heating, taxes, and insurance. Quite often, unscrupulous landlords will try to collect more than 100 percent of their costs from the combined pass-alongs they charge their tenants—by obscuring the actual square footage.

Your lease should be assignable and should further represent that the location may be used for "any legal use" or for "general use" by a business similar to your own. This will mean that you can assign the lease to another business easily, if you move for any reason or want to sell. Otherwise, the landlord can, in effect, hold you hostage. If you are a retailer without an assignable lease it is absolutely impossible to sell the business.

Don't ignore the need for lease assignability simply because you don't plan on selling. You are building something that may last longer than you, and then again, it may not. Your family may not want to continue running the business after you die. Likewise, you may need to retire and sell at some point. Even though you are an entrepreneur, that doesn't mean you are indestructible or immortal.

Any rights that the landlord has to cancel the lease, even for money, should be carefully scrutinized by you and your attorney. Make sure that there are specific reasons given for cancellation and that you receive adequate remuneration based upon future values.

Rent increases must be described fully, in terms of both amount and timing. These are totally negotiable. Try not to pay rent until after the space is fixed up.

An occupancy date should be provided in every commercial lease. If the space isn't delivered as promised by that date you should have the right to terminate the agreement.

If the landlord wants a rent that you can't afford right now, try to negotiate a graduated lease. The average rent can be to the landlord's liking, and the initial lower payments can help you make it in the early going.

Leasing does have its drawbacks. Any improvements you make to the facility—and often these are substantial—become the property of your landlord. Remember this when choosing locations that seem inexpensive. Put as little of your own money into renovating the space as possible—try to get the landlord to pick up the costs. It is actually better to take space that's more expensive if the landlord will cover renovation costs. Often a landlord will renovate and spread the cost over the term of the lease—this could be a very cheap form of borrowing for the entrepreneur.

Now that you have determined the location of your business and negotiated your lease you can begin to plan how to get customers to come there through marketing and promotion, the subjects of the next chapter.

CHAPTER SEVEN

Cultivating the Right Image for Your Business

The codfish lays ten thousand eggs
The homely hen lays one.
The codfish never cackles
To tell you what she's done.
And so we scorn the codfish,
While the humble hen we prize,
Which only goes to show you
That it pays to advertise.
—ANONYMOUS

Entrepreneurs, like most creative people, are extremely self-centered. They believe that everyone can see what they are doing, or recognize their intelligence, skill, and worth. They believe that if they build that proverbial better mousetrap, the world actually will beat a path to their door. Unfortunately, they—and the writer of that proverb—are nearly always dead wrong.

Businesses do not succeed through spontaneous combustion. Marketing isn't automatic. You can combine all the necessary elements in your business, but without the spark of the marketing effort, it won't catch fire. You have to either bring the customer to your business, or bring your business to the customer. They won't do it on their own. Sure, your family and friends will frequent your new enterprise, and maybe they'll even tell their friends. You may even get a sprinkling of innovators (as marketers refer to those rare customers who are always willing to try something new). But that can never be enough for you to succeed, or even break even. For a business to flourish it will have to bring in strangers. You can have a wonderful idea, find a fabulous location, do your market research, and establish that you really do address a need, but unless you tell the world about it, all your efforts will be for naught.

Remember, an incredible amount of pre-purchase dissonant noise is being generated out there by hundreds and thousands of other business people—and that's just in your immediate area. Extend that over a metropolitan area, a state, and then the country, and you can get a sense of the overwhelming din the consumer must deal with. With all that competition for the consumer's attention, it isn't surprising that you'll have to scream and jump up and down a bit to get noticed.

If the public is your quarry and you scrimped on location, you'll end up taking all you saved and throwing it into your marketing—at least if you want to succeed. It really comes down to a choice: Pay for a high-traffic location in the first place or pay for high-visibility marketing that may bring consumers to your cheaper, out-of-the-way location. Even if you opted for a strong location, you'll still have to spend on marketing. There are few businesses that can succeed with walk-in trade alone.

Your marketing also plays a vital role in all the plans you make. If you need to break even by a certain point for your projections to work out, then your marketing and promotion plan had better insure that enough customers will come in. That can be tough, especially for a small business. Major corporations routinely allocate 1 or 2 percent of their gross to the marketing effort. You may need to put as much as 10 percent of your anticipated gross into marketing and promotion. The only ironclad rule about marketing costs is that you have to spend whatever it takes to get the job done.

When I was a venture capitalist, I used to be taken aback if I saw a large amount of money allocated to marketing in a business plan. I didn't know any better. Today's financial people are a bit more sophisticated than I was. They know that in order to make money you have to spend money on pulling customers in. Good business plans now usually include a marketing plan. You have to show that you can hit your targeted customers and bring enough of them in to break even and then turn a profit. And, as hard as it may sound now, you must show how long it will take. I'll explain how that's done in Chapter Twelve: The Anatomy of a Business Plan.

Additionally, the public image of your business includes anything you do to make yourself *and* your business appear more attractive or professional, and anything you do to encourage a potential customer to make a purchase. Even your pricing policy fits into this category. Each business has its own needs and resources, so coming up with the right mix of these elements, and outlining it in a business plan, will be a custom job for your business.

When examining your marketing options it's important to keep in mind the type of business you have, the nature of your customer, and the profit margin of your product. Look for all the different ways you can reach the user of your product. These are called distribution channels. Remember it isn't necessary for you to sell directly to the end user. It may be more cost effective to market to other businesses who already sell to the user—or even to sell to a distributor, who in turn sells to retailers. And this choice of distribution pattern will have a dramatic effect on your marketing costs. If you are selling to other businesses, or if you are selling a big-ticket item, you may have to concentrate your efforts in a sales force. If, on the other hand, you are selling to the general public, or offering products with a low markup, you may want to concentrate on advertising.

In Chapters Eighteen and Nineteen we will look at specific marketing techniques and strategies for retail and service businesses, but for now, let's go over some general rules.

When you mention the words marketing and promotion to most entrepreneurs they immediately think of advertising campaigns, direct mail, and other overt selling efforts. Actually, the key marketing efforts of the beginning entrepreneur make up what I like to call the "skin" of the business—his or her own appearance and visible attitude; the appearance and manners of the staff; stationery and business cards; packaging and merchandising; answering machine messages; the cleanliness, design, and lighting of the business site; window displays; and signs—any part of yourself or your business that is exposed to the outside world. For the start-up business these are clearly more important than the more traditional marketing techniques—most entrepreneurs aren't going to be able to throw many dollars around in the early stages.

Classicism and traditionalism are the keys to putting the best "skin" on a business. Remember, something becomes classic because it has worked for years and years.

There should be nothing about you or your business that could trigger negative feelings in potential customers. That means that your stationery should probably be traditional. Logos and signs can also be extremely important. A logo sends customers a message about your business. Your face and smile can't be everywhere—that's why you need a logo. It will be on your stationery, on shopping bags—everywhere it will fit. If it is unique, fun, intelligent, or intriguing, so much the better. Signs aren't going to bring herds of new customers to your store, but they can have a cumulative, almost subliminal effectiveness. Savvy entrepreneurs use colorful banners in tandem with signs, giving their business exposure in all directions.

The message on your answering machine should be businesslike. Forget music and jokes, just play it straight. Likewise, your clothing and manner should be traditional—you should appear both non-threatening and pleasant. Your phone should be answered promptly and courteously. Long delays, being put on hold, or dealing with rude, gum-chewing receptionists isn't going to turn on your customers. Tell everyone who works for you to smile. It's amazing what a difference a smile makes.

You and your staff should be neat, clean, and businesslike in appearance. Teach your employees how to treat customers. Politeness and charm are two of the most effective marketing tools available. When someone comes into my office I smile, bend a bit at the waist—a sort of semi-bow—and shake hands, a practice I learned from my father. I ask if they'd like coffee or tea. Before they leave I ask if they need to use the bathroom or make a phone call. I am making obvious my care and concern for their well-being. Showing that you care is the speediest way to instill trust in customers or clients.

Don't think that customers will be drawn to you despite a slovenly or "eccentric" appearance. The first impression we have of someone is based—rightly or wrongly—on appearance, so yours had better be acceptable to *everyone*. Retailers should never ask customers "Can I help you?"—that places pressure on them. Instead, gently say, "If you need help just ask." In everything you do, create trust by showing your customers that you care about them.

Obviously, the way your place of business looks creates a response in customers. People hate to go into a place that looks shabby. Refuse and dust imply poor merchandise or service. Piles of paper mean wasteful and ineffective service. A place of business should be well-lit, sparkling, and inviting. Don't underestimate odors either. Any offensive smell is guaranteed to turn off potential customers. Have fresh flowers around—they add immeasurably to both the odor and appearance of a store or office.

The way you display your wares tells the customer how much value you place on them. Products displayed with care and taste just seem to jump off the shelves into customers' arms. Everything must look and feel fresh—whether it is per-ishable or not. If that means you have to throw out aging products, so be it. Fresh merchandise is essential for bringing customers back.

For manufacturers, good product packaging is vital. Packages not only provide information, but can enhance your product's aesthetic appeal as well. One interesting trend today is toward multi-purpose packaging. For example, preserves can be sold in reusable decorative jars. Your packages should be stackable and noticeable. Remember: The more impressive your packaging, the better placement you'll receive in stores. Any special packaging you can provide—such as countertop displays, carousels, or racks—will help get your product better exposure.

I recently went into a housewares shop that did a remarkable interior display job. It was Christmas season, and the owner had piles of gaily pre-wrapped presents with the item inside displayed on top of the pile. It was wonderful. The boxes looked absolutely lovely, and were selling like hotcakes. The packaging, the display, and the fact that she had done the wrapping for the customer really added to the item's appeal.

The window of a retail store should be alluring and interesting—an invitation for customers to enter. You are paying a premium for space with frontage on a street, so you had better use it to your advantage. It is remarkable what a good window display can do for a retail store. If you need any proof, look at the lines of potential customers staring at department store window displays just before Christmas.

A large part of my wife's job is to find new, exciting merchandise on sale in New York City for *New York* magazine. She has discovered that a store's insides match its outsides. She can spot sickness in a store right away by examining its window displays. A haphazard window display, or one that never changes, indicates an ailing, or simply boring, store. A store that my wife and I used to frequent changed ownership recently. The original owner, the entrepreneur who started the business, was always rearranging his window display. It was exciting to see what new items were in the store. All that changed when he sold out. The window displays became routine—and so did the store. People stopped dropping in.

Rather than spark up his windows, the new owner launched an expensive newspaper advertising campaign. It failed miserably. A thriving business had been run into the ground, at least partly because of poor window marketing.

Customers hesitate to walk into an empty place of business. If there are no customers inside, circulate, clean up, and rearrange your merchandise. If there's a staff, have them do likewise. If you are in the restaurant business, put your first customers near the window so that others won't feel uncomfortable about entering.

Next, let's look at the three main ways you can encourage potential customers to buy from you: sales staff, advertising, and publicity.

SALES STAFF AND REPRESENTATIVES

Whatever promotional mix you come up with, the foundation of your effort will be salespeople. The main functions of sales personnel are to find potential customers, make a sales presentation, obtain an order, and follow up and service the customer. If your promotional campaign concentrates on personal selling, it will be important to have sales personnel who can fulfill all these functions. But if you are using advertising to find customers and make sales presentations then all you may need are order takers.

The best salesman I know is Kenny Tillman, owner of S&S Sound City, a consumer electronics store in New York City. He radiates love and caring and concern. He seems to know every customer's first name. When Kenny shows you a product he almost caresses it. He personalizes sales, saying things like "these speakers aren't for you, but the pair over there are perfect." Customers instinctively trust him. His store is surrounded by competitors who all charge similar prices, yet Kenny has an extremely loyal clientele. To a large degree his customers are buying him, as much as his products.

Many entrepreneurs, like Kenny Tillman, take on the role of salesperson, building up the business through their personal contacts, skill, and drive. But as time goes on, and the business matures, it may become impossible for the entrepreneur to do this job well. (As we will see in Chapter Ten: The

Pains of Unbundling, many new responsibilities and roles await the successful small business person.) When that happens, the entrepreneur must take on the role of sales manager—and either hire a sales staff or farm the job out to independent sales representatives.

If sales personnel will be on staff, the entrepreneur will be responsible for hiring, teaching, managing, and paying them. Finding and hiring sales personnel isn't an easy job. But who better to know the personality and skills necessary to make a sale than the successful entrepreneur who has already sold the product? Teaching may involve taking new salespeople out in the field, or putting them behind the counter, exposing them to the rigors and rejections of sales. If the products are highly technical there will be a need for continuing rigorous education. Retailers and wholesalers may find that their suppliers are willing to help train and educate their salespeople. Managing the sales force will require the entrepreneur to set priorities for his or her salespeople, showing them how best to allocate their time and energies. This can only be accomplished once your market and customer studies are completed. Compensation for salespeople generally involves salary, commission on sales, or a combination of both. While each business may have its own unusual circumstances, it's accepted wisdom that a combination of salary and commission works best, since it offers both security and incentive. Happiness is contagious. A happy sales staff will create more happy, satisfied customers.

Kenny Tillman has successfully cloned himself. Today, S&S Sound City is filled with dozens of mini-Kennys who radiate the same warmth and caring that he does. They are well paid and love their jobs—and it shows, both in their attitude toward customers and in their affection for the store.

Rather than spend time acquiring and training an in-house sales staff, many entrepreneurs bring in independent sales representatives. This means that the only training necessary will be product-specific instruction, and that many of the sales management responsibilities will be taken care of by someone else. In addition, good sales reps already have contacts in the industry, speeding up your new product's or service's acceptance by customers.

Charcoal Companion's Charles Adams decided to use independent reps to sell his barbecue products to retailers. "I've found that reps can work ten or twelve non-competitive lines with integrity—any more than that and some will be given poor representation," he notes. Adams calls these representatives "the shepherds of our reputation" and stresses the importance of choosing top people. "When we began looking for reps we decided to work backward. We called up the best retailers in a territory and asked them who were the top independent reps they dealt with," Adams recalls. "The same names would keep cropping up. We then courted the reps—selling them on our products—and checked if there were any conflicts. That's how we ended up with a great sales force."

ADVERTISING

Advertising is the most effective promotional device for reaching a great many people in a short period of time. It may be as important as any other aspect of your business. That doesn't mean every business must advertise, only that they all have to weigh the benefits against the costs. Necessary or not, advertising remains the most difficult and dangerous part of the promotional package. Every business has unique advertising needs. Therefore, a careful study of your market research, dollar projections, and the advertising avenues available is essential.

Go back to your analysis of potential customers and pay careful attention to who they are, which of their needs you are meeting, and what advantages your product or service has over the competition. Ask yourself, "Why am I advertising?" Is it to generate awareness of your business and its products? Is it to unveil a new product? Is it to sway customers from a competitor's offerings to your own? Whatever the reason, your goal must be clearly stated, for it is this goal that will determine the type of advertising you do and its content.

The next step in developing an advertising effort is to come up with your budget. The best method is to treat advertising as part of the cost of doing business. Consider your advertising, whatever its frequency or price, as an annualized cost. Advertising should never be under-capitalized. That will only lead to its failure.

Research whether cooperative advertising funds are available in your industry. Many manufacturers, for example, will provide funds for retailers to place their own ads touting the vendor's products. You may also be able to take advantage of advertising combines made up of businesses that have some aspect in common—location, for example.

Deciding when to advertise is just as important as coming up with a budget. Again, go back to your market research. Does the business you are entering have seasonal ups and downs? Do customers buy the products or services regularly, or does the purchase have to be encouraged? How often can the customer be expected to make a purchase? Packaged goods companies, generally, must advertise right away to launch a new product. But it can be self-destructive for a business to advertise too soon. One of the worst things you can do is advertise and not be able to handle the demand you've created. Those customers you turn away will never return.

The three most common advertising patterns are: advertising during peak seasons, advertising during off-seasons, and constant advertising. For example, if your customers buy regularly, it's important to advertise heavily before peak buying periods, but also to keep a steady advertising presence all year.

Next, examine the advertising media available to you with an eye toward reach, frequency, demographics, and cost. Reach is the number of people who see the message and frequency is the number of times they see it. If you are looking to create awareness you go for a broad reach; frequency, on the other hand, creates sales.

Here's a brief look at a variety of advertising media, their advantages and their disadvantages:

• Newspaper advertising reaches a great many people, many times, and at an affordable cost. That's what makes it a favorite of start-up businesses. Yet it's possible for an ad to be lost in a newspaper—and it's difficult to tell if your customers are among those being reached. Newspapers aren't necessarily good for strategic advertising—creating an image—but they are one of the best sources for tactical advertising. If you are holding a sale there is no better medium.

• Magazine advertising reaches specific audiences and has a long life—yet it is expensive and easy for potential customers to overlook. There are so many specialized magazines around that it shouldn't be difficult for a small business to find one that it could afford on a regular basis.

• Directories—such as the Yellow Pages—reach customers who have already made a decision to buy and have a long life span. But an ad can get lost among the competition.

• Direct mail can be an extremely effective tool for businesses. It is selective, fast-acting and can have exactly as broad a reach as the entrepreneur wishes. With direct mail, it is possible for entrepreneurs to either pinpoint their efforts or use a broad brush. Unfortunately, it is expensive and there is no way to guarantee that your audience will pay attention to your message. People don't open all their mail. For your direct mail message to work it will have to be grabbing and original. If you are in an urban area, try delivering promotional pieces to apartment or office buildings rather than paying for the postage.

• Trade shows and conventions can be very effective for manufacturers and wholesalers looking to target retailers and distributors. But it can cost a small fortune to attend one, considering today's travel, entertainment, lodging, and display costs.

• Billboards and transit advertising are inexpensive, considering the number of people they reach—yet they allow only a short message.

• Television has a tremendous reach and can make a dramatic impression—but it's expensive, and it's tough to tell if your customers are among those watching. Even major advertising executives admit that there is no sure way to know that your TV ad is really reaching your potential customers.

• Radio spots reach a great many people, are affordable, and let you target a specific audience. But radio can be the toughest advertising to do well—you'll probably need help from the stations you choose, or from an agency.

• Private sale advertising can be extremely effective in creating and maintaining a stable of loyal repeat customers. A mailing—or a series of telephone calls—to a solid customer list, offering a special "regular customer only" price, is an excellent way to firm up your business's foundation of support.

Once you've determined your advertising goals, budget, and media, give thought to the message you'd like to convey to your customers. Every advertising message, to be effective, must get the target's attention, hold it, address a need, and foster an action, in that order. Failure to achieve just one part of this equation will result in an ineffective ad. Examine the competition's advertising message and try to find an opening for your own, different message. Advertising agencies can be a real help in this area, but depending on your budget, the assistance may be too costly.

Devise some way of tracking the effectiveness of your advertising. Compare your stated goal with the actual results. Among the best techniques are coupons, "mention this ad" discounts or rewards, and inquiries.

There are five major advertising mistakes that entrepreneurs make: not spending enough, spending too much, not being ready for sales, poor positioning, and not knowing their customer. Advertising is a great tool—when it's used properly. There is an old advertising adage: "Half of all advertising is wasted—but no one knows which half."

PUBLICITY

Publicity is free exposure for a business. It is essential for any start-up and can take the form of sponsorships, news coverage in the media, or community service. Since many customers believe that advertising is, by its very nature, slanted, they may not believe your message. Publicity, on the other hand, is accepted more readily—since it doesn't have a hard sell attached. Once something appears in print, customers tend to accept it as gospel. Just remember that one-shot publicity won't be effective. To make a dent in the market you will need a steady stream of publicity that reinforces your message. This type of cumulative campaign can pay enormous dividends.

Publicity can be one of the most effective forms of promotion. The din of advertising in a major metropolitan area, for example, nearly deafens the consumer. As a result, that consumer often reaches out to third parties—word of mouth, or expert opinion, for example—to help make choices.

Every Little Leaguer who wears your business's name on his or her back is a walking advertisement, not only of your product or service, but of your goodwill and character as well. Each mention in the press, referring to you either as an expert or as a concerned member of the community, serves to boost your business's image. Never underestimate the power of the printed word. And never pass up a chance to publicize your involvement in the community. Any charitable contribution, any sponsorship, any talk before a local organization, any class taught, can add to your bottom line.

Speeches can be terrific publicity devices for entrepreneurs in service businesses. Not only is it possible to get new clients from among those listening to the speech, but your name and credentials may well be printed in a program or newsletter that is widely circulated. If you are part of a panel, the interaction with other experts can lead to referrals and consultations. Don't expect to get instant results from your speechmaking. Experts have found that it may take as long as three years for all the potential new clients to find your office. That's another good reason to make your publicity efforts a continuing part of your marketing program.

Word of mouth remains the best way to attract customers, and the only method of spreading it is to actively encourage pleased customers to tell their friends. There are shopping "patrons" out there—individuals who look at shopping as their hobby. These people "collect" new stores and new businesses the way others collect art. Once you've reached them, these people get a thrill from introducing others to a business they've "discovered."

As you can tell, I am enamored of public relations—but not of public relations people. Public relations professionals can help get your business attention, but they can be expensive and the results are often mixed. If you can afford to hire publicists, make sure they have experience in your industry and contacts with the major media. They should know whom to contact, how best to do it, and what type of information to offer. For most fledgling business people, however, "publicity manager" will have to become one more part of their own job description.

There are thousands of television and radio stations and tens of thousands of newspapers and magazines in this country, all starved for useful information. If you can provide them with it you will become a regular contact, someone quoted often and referred to as an "expert." This is especially true if you are in a service business.

Lori and Dana Pollan and Caren Austin of the Pollan-Austin Fitness Center became publicity experts to help promote their business. The three young women spent time each day handing out flyers in their neighborhood. Clad in their leotards, they passed brochures out at the subway station in their area. But they also cultivated a relationship with the press. "We soon discovered that by being accessible, reliable, and predictable we could count on continued publicity," Dana Pollan notes. "And once we began being contacted for our opinions our reputations as experts grew," Lori adds. Their notoriety has reached the point where they no longer have to go out after publicity—it comes to them. Major magazines now contact them monthly and use them as a barometer of their industry.

PRICE AS A MARKETING TOOL

Pricing is a double-edged sword. The price you place on your product or service, in addition to covering your costs and providing for profit, plays a vital role in customer perception. It is, therefore, an important part of your business's image as well as its finances. This makes pricing one of the most complicated issues facing the entrepreneur. I'll get into the financial ramifications of pricing in Chapter Fourteen: Financial Management, but for now, let's examine its marketing implications.

Your price should reflect what potential customers believe to be the value of your product or service—which, if you are selling to retailers, includes their ability to resell it—not what *you* believe to be its value.

Mary Gilroy, owner of the vintage clothing store Molly Bloom, once put a lovely little bouquet of dried flowers on sale. Her pricing policy was based primarily on image, rather than on her costs (most of her merchandise was obtained at little or no cost), and she "felt" that a price of $7.50 was appropriate. The bouquet sat in the store for months. Finally, she decided to raise the price from $7.50 to $17.50. It sold that day. The flowers suddenly took on a higher perceived value just because they were priced higher.

The marketing aspects of pricing are vexing for most entrepreneurs. Quite a few make mistakes based on their impatience or insecurity.

The most common error entrepreneurs make is undercharging. Believing that selling a product for less will bring success quickly can be fatal for a small business. Generally, larger, more established businesses will have lower production costs than small start-up businesses. In addition, larger businesses can take advantage of volume discounts that the small business can't match. Small service businesses will have the same overhead, or costs, regardless of the volume of sales they achieve. That means that in the early stages of the business they will have high costs associated with each sale. Their larger, more established competitors will have lower costs associated with each sale. In both product and service businesses, therefore, large, established businesses will be better able to sell at lower prices than small start-ups. Discount pricing, for a start-up business, will lead not to rapid success but to rapid failure.

Another mistake frequently made by start-up businesses is to undercharge due to fear. This is particularly true in service businesses. Entrepreneurs who often provide the service themselves, may feel that their lack of experience forces them to charge low prices. It is also seen as a way to get customers quickly. But undercharging this way does more harm than good. First, it is next to impossible to start with low prices and then raise them. If at some point the entrepreneur finds that it is essential to lower prices, that can be done easily. Raising prices, on the other hand, is likely to result in disgruntled customers who soon become former customers.

The price you set on your product or service helps create your image in the mind of the customer. If you set your price too low, or charge less than what your competitors charge, customers may believe that what you are offering isn't as valuable as the alternatives. And it is impossible to overcome this perception.

I once counseled a professional security person, a former FBI agent, who provides security services for celebrities. I asked him how much he charged for his services. He said that he's been charging $150 an hour for the past ten years. I was shocked. He was selling the most precious commodity in the world. He could have been charging his clients $400 an hour and they wouldn't have batted an eye. In fact, he probably would have gotten more business. He didn't realize the perceived value of his services.

Keeping in mind that prices must always exceed the costs of production, let's look at the implications of the three traditional pricing/marketing approaches: comparable pricing, low pricing, and high pricing.

If you set your prices at the same level as your competition you will have little or no chance of success. Remember that you are the new person on the block. The existing businesses will already have built customer bases. If you offer the same product or service at the same price, what possible reason will customers have to switch from their existing supplier? And if you offer a better product or service at the same price as the others in the market you are undercharging. We have already discussed the problems that will create.

Low-price marketing requires entrepreneurs to set their selling price just above their cost in an effort to get a large number of sales in a short period of time. This can be effective in selling unique products that are easily duplicated. By entering the market at a low price entrepreneurs can grab a large share of the potential market very quickly. Unfortunately, once the product or service is duplicated by someone else the business can degenerate into a downward cycle of discounts. This plays right into the hands of large businesses, who can afford to sustain a period of losses, and spells disaster for small businesses. If you believe that your product or service has a short life-cycle, low pricing may work. Just be prepared to come up with another product or service if you want your business to last.

In general, the best pricing/marketing approach for small businesses to follow is charging a higher price. This automatically reinforces the difference between you and your competitors. It conveys quality and status, maximizes sales and profits, and helps recover start-up costs more quickly. Remember, it is easier to lower prices than to raise them. Once you have gathered your initial base of customers you may need to lower prices to broaden that base or respond to competition.

PRICING DECISIONS

Once you have determined which of these pricing approaches to take you'll have to settle on a strategy. Your objective is to make your product or service as attractive to potential customers as possible. That's why you should take consumer psychology into account in making your decisions.

Consumers generally expect prices to be either *odd* or *even*. An odd price is one in which the last digit is an odd number, traditionally, a 9. For example: $9.99. While there really is no evidence to back it up, business people who sell products assume that consumers will perceive odd prices as being lower than even prices. The product selling for $19.99 is perceived as being a better value than the one selling for $20.00, even though the difference is only $.01. Service businesses, on the other hand, invariably charge even prices—$20, as opposed to $19.99. The odd pricing of a service tends to create an image of lower quality rather than of higher value. Some product businesses take advantage of this perception by keeping all their prices at round numbers—$100, for example. This works well when coupled with a high-price marketing approach.

Your pricing will be either *flexible* or *firm*. Flexible pricing means that customers can negotiate the price down. This can help increase sales in the short term. Sales that might otherwise not have occurred can be closed. In the long term, however, this strategy can lead to problems. Customers who failed to negotiate will become angry if they discover that your pricing was flexible. In addition, customers are never sure that they got the most for their money; they'll always wonder if they could have dickered you down a few more dollars. Flexible pricing *never* works in service businesses. As soon as the entrepreneur indicates that the price is negotiable the perceived value of the service decreases. In general, firm pricing works best.

There are, however, other ways to increase sales volume through pricing: establishing good, better, and best lines; promotional pricing; and discounting.

Good-better-best pricing is a common retail strategy. An electronics store, for example, might offer three types of televisions: a full-featured high price model; a stripped-down low price model; and a third model somewhere in the middle. This strategy appeals to all customers: the price-conscious, the value-conscious, and the quality-conscious. In effect, you will be able to broaden your marketing strategy to reach a wider range of market segments. This can also help simplify inventory purchasing and selling. The trick to this strategy is to set the prices far enough apart that the customer can perceive the differences, yet close enough together to appeal to borderline market segments. Service businesses, however, run a risk in offering a range of differently priced services. The customer will question whether the lowest-price service is adequate and if the highest-price service is really worth the extra dollars.

Promotional pricing is the practice of offering one particular product or service at or below cost in order to attract customers who, you hope, will also purchase other, higher-priced products or services. As long as the promotionally priced sale leads to sufficient sales of regularly priced items this strategy can work. But be careful—it can be difficult to raise the price of a promotional item. If the promotional item is the only thing drawing customers to your business your success will be short-lived.

Discounting is the third method of boosting sales volume through pricing. This strategy requires the purchaser to perform some service to the business in exchange for a lower price. Typically, discounts are based on the method of payment or the number of products purchased.

Offering a discount to a customer who pays a bill within a certain period of time can help insure cash flow. A classic example of this type of discounting is known as "2/10, net 30." This means that if the customer pays the bill within ten days of the purchase he or she can take a 2 percent discount off the price. If the bill is not paid within ten days the total amount is due within thirty days.

Offering a discount to a customer who purchases a large amount helps cut down overhead costs. The cost per sale for each item drops dramatically. By extending this volume discount to a period of time (for example: the customer must purchase ten thousand widgets in a year) the entrepreneur locks the customer in as a regular, valuable source of business.

FORGING A UNIFIED PROMOTIONAL PLAN

Since there is no single foolproof promotional technique, every successful business will divide its resources, trying to come up with the most effective mix. Good planning can maximize the effectiveness of each technique, insuring that your potential customers are reached, persuaded, and urged to act. Many businesses take a haphazard approach to promotion, taking an ad when the newspaper salesperson calls, or adding sales staff when demand has already grown. Instead, plan your promotional efforts on a calendar basis.

Coming up with a unified promotional plan was an adventure for Charles Adams, vice-president of Charcoal Companion. At first, Adams and his partner, Doug Fielding, thought that the best method for promoting their charcoal lighter was television advertising. They shot their own thirty-second commercial in the backyard. It cost $3,000—one-tenth of their capital. They paid for a toll-free phone number, as well as Visa and Mastercard services, for the responses they assumed would be pouring in. Then they bought spots on local independent stations—a package of fourteen spots over ten days at a variety of times—for $3,500. The total cost of the program was $8,000. Unfortunately, they got only fifty phone calls and grossed only $400.

After licking their wounds, Adams and Fielding pressed ahead. "It wasn't a defeat, it was a lesson. It taught us that there are elements in business that aren't always obvious," Adams relates. "The trip from manufacturer to consumer was longer than we thought. We learned that selling the consumer wasn't all there was, and redirected our efforts to selling the retailer."

The duo re-worked their business plan, incorporated, approached family and friends for investments, and picked up approximately $50,000 worth of equity financing. With their coffers a bit more healthy, they then set up a network of sales reps, offering commissions only.

Now addressing an audience of only two thousand customers—the universe of possible retailers of their products—Adams and Fielding produced beautiful, glossy catalogs for use as a sales aid. The brochure cost $12,500 to produce, but it has been worth every penny. "Samples aren't really an issue now, and we can sell different products to different types of stores. We have lines for mass merchants, department stores, and specialty stores," Adams notes.

Adams and his company are careful to keep the psychology of their customer—the retailer—in mind. They under- rather than over-sell, preferring that retailers run out, and call for more, rather than find some of their products sitting on the shelves unsold. Their product was priced higher than its competitors, but offered greater long-term value to consumers.

Charcoal Companion backed up its efforts at selling retailers with a public relations campaign. Adams put together a publicity package and sent it to fifteen hundred magazine and newspaper editors. It got them lots of exposure in major publications—and the third-party endorsements from experts made it even more effective than advertising. Rather than buying the space through advertising, they created the space through public relations.

As your business matures your marketing efforts will have to evolve. Products and services go through life cycles. Early on, innovative ideas must be targeted at a certain type of customer. As the idea becomes accepted, the target customer base must be broadened. At some point, every idea's market becomes saturated—there's no one new left to sell. Then, the idea must be redirected, either by showing a new use for it or by improving it. Each of these steps in the product's life cycle will require different marketing strategies and promotional mixes. It is no wonder that most successful entrepreneurs either start out as, or become, marketing geniuses.

Even if you put together an effective promotional mix, as Charcoal Companion did, and back that up with a professional image, that doesn't guarantee your success as an entrepreneur. So far we've covered just the first steps on the entrepreneurial path. You can come up with the right idea, research your market, accurately gauge your break-even, find an excellent location, plan a great promotional effort, and still fail if you don't have enough seed capital behind you.

CHAPTER EIGHT

Finding Seed
Financing

Business? It's quite simple.
It's other people's money.
—ALEXANDER DUMAS THE YOUNGER

The single most difficult and often most stressful aspect of going into your own business is raising the seed capital—the money needed to plan, prepare, open, and run the business until it breaks even. Despite all claims to the contrary, institutional lenders and investors are *not* going to provide seed capital for your business. Banks may run ads about how they have helped small business people get started, but what they really mean is that they helped small businesses expand. A small business does not become bankable until it has a track record. And that goes for venture capitalists and Small Business Investment Companies, as well as commercial banks. The only places to find real seed capital are your own pocket, friends, relatives, a home equity loan, potential partners, sympathetic suppliers—and perhaps an "angel."

But before you begin looking for start-up money you have to make sure that your personal financial responsibilities are taken care of. Starting a business will require your total commitment—body and soul. You'll be working long hours, dealing with hundreds of details, and sweating over thousands of decisions. That will require a 100 percent effort—any less and your chance for success is dramatically reduced. You can't start a business successfully and worry about where your next meal will come from or how your daughter's medical bills will be paid.

That means, ideally, you should have enough money in the bank to cover eighteen months of your personal expenses, above and beyond the money needed to start the business. You'll probably know after only six months whether the business will make it. But it may well take another year after that for the business to become profitable enough for you to draw a salary. Pare expenses to a minimum, working out a personal austerity budget. With your next eighteen months taken care of, you can take the next step—calculating how much seed money you'll need.

There are two parts to this calculation: determining how much cash you will need for your start-up costs and figuring out how much working capital you'll need to get you to the break-even point.

Typical start-up costs include: deposits for rent, telephone, utility and insurance; any machinery and equipment;

office equipment, furniture, stationery, and supplies; transportation equipment; professional fees for creating a business structure, negotiating leases, and financial planning; advance advertising and publicity costs; leasehold improvements; and at least one turnover of your inventory. The amount you list for each of these items should reflect the initial cash outlay. If any of them will be paid off over time, include the deposit, but reflect the monthly payments in your overhead—this part of your start-up costs will become part of your working capital requirements.

Next, calculate how much you will have to spend each month to operate the business—your working capital requirement. This can be determined by drawing up a budget and cash flow analysis, something I will go over in detail in Chapter Fourteen: Financial Management. For now, let's look at a simplified scenario: In the early stages of the business you will have to spend more money than you take in. You will need enough working capital each month to make up the difference between what you spend and what you receive. With each passing month, your business should be taking in more and more money, leaving you with less and less need for cash working capital. At some point, one hopes, you will take in as much money in one month as you have to spend. This is your cash break-even point. After this point, you will begin to take in more money than you have to spend, creating a cash surplus, which is the same as a cash profit.

The total amount of cash you need to keep the business operating until it breaks even is the amount of working capital you'll need to start the business. Add this to your total start-up costs and you have a good approximation of the amount of seed money you'll need to launch the business.

The most common mistake entrepreneurs make in calculating their seed money requirements is to overestimate their gross receipts—the money they will be taking in each month. Invariably, entrepreneurs project that they will be bringing in more money than they actually do. To compensate for this, be very conservative in your projections of gross receipts. Work up a modest-case scenario. If you don't break even by the point you project you will have to find additional financing.

The tables on pages 124–130 provide a brief look at the

MANUFACTURING BUSINESSES—START-UP COSTS IN DOLLARS

Type of Cost	Total Assets 10,000–100,000	Total Assets 100,000–250,000	Total Assets 250,000–500,000	Total Assets 500,000–1,000,000
Deposits				
Rent	1,700–10,000	3,300–15,000	5,000–20,000	6,700–25,000
Telephone	500–800	800–1,000	1,000–1,300	1,300–2,500
Utilities	700–1,300	1,300–2,000	2,000–2,700	2,700–3,300
Insurance	1,400–2,100	2,100–2,800	2,800–3,500	3,500–4,200
Furniture & Off. Equip.				
Desks, chairs	2,900–3,400	3,900–4,400	5,300–5,800	6,800–7,800
Safe	1,000–2,000	1,000–2,000	1,000–2,000	1,000–2,000
Typewriters	1,000–2,400	1,500–3,600	2,000–4,800	2,500–6,000
Computers	3,000–7,500	3,000–7,500	5,000–15,000	5,000–15,000
Phone system	500–5,000	500–5,000	2,500–7,500	3,500–10,000
Copy machine	800–2,000	800–4,000	1,500–6,500	3,000–13,000
Fax machine	1,000–3,500	1,000–3,500	1,000–3,500	1,000–3,500
File cabinets	400–800	800–1,200	1,200–1,600	1,600–2,000
Misc. furniture	1,000–2,000	2,000–3,000	3,000–4,000	4,000–5,000
Off. supplies	5,600–7,800	5,600–7,800	6,200–12,500	6,200–12,500
Mach. & Equip.	1,000–24,000	10,000–60,000	25,000–120,000	50,000–240,000
Transportation Equip.				
Van	12,000–20,000	12,000–20,000	12,000–20,000	12,000–20,000
Delivery truck	20,000–25,000	20,000–25,000	35,000–40,000	55,000–80,000
Leasehold Imp.	7,500–28,000	11,300–42,000	15,000–52,500	22,500–87,500
(General Contractor)				

Prof. Fees	1,500–4,000	1,500–4,000	3,500–7,500
Advertising	3,000–10,000	3,000–10,000	3,000–10,000
Working Capital	5,100–30,000	15,000–60,000	20,100–75,000
Inventory	1,300–23,000	32,500–115,000	65,000–230,000
Totals	72,900–214,600	180,300–513,200	279,900–861,800

Assumptions—Manufacturing Businesses

1. Deposits: Rent: 2,000–4,000 sq. ft., 4,000–6,000 sq. ft., 6,000–8,000 sq. ft., 8,000–10,000 sq. ft.; $5–$15 / sq. ft.; 2 months deposit— Telephone: $250 / line—Utilities: $4 / ft.; 1–2 months deposit.
2. Furniture & Office Equipment: Desks cost $300 each; chairs cost $100 each; credenzas cost $500 each; bookcases cost $400 each.
3. Machinery & Equipment: Represents a nationwide average of between 10 and 24 percent of total assets.
4. Transportation Equipment: Average of quotes for vans, 10-ft. trucks ($20,000–$25,000) and 24-ft. trucks ($35,000–$40,000).
5. Leasehold Improvements: $15–$35 / sq. ft. on office space ranging from 500 to 2,500 sq. ft.
6. Working Capital: 6 months rent.
7. Inventory: Represents a nationwide average of 13–23 percent of total assets.

WHOLESALE BUSINESSES—START-UP COSTS IN DOLLARS

Type of Cost	No Warehouse	Lt. Warehouse	Hvy. Warehouse
Deposits			
Rent	1,700–5,000	4,200–12,500	8,300–25,000
Telephone	500–1,000	1,000–1,500	1,000–2,000
Utilities	400–800	800–1,600	1,700–3,400
Insurance	700–1,400	1,400–2,100	2,100–2,800
Furniture & Off. Equip.			
Desks, chairs	1,900–2,300	3,200–4,000	4,500–5,300
Safe	1,000–2,000	1,000–2,000	1,000–2,000
Typewriters	500–1,200	1,000–2,400	1,500–3,600
Computers	3,000–7,500	5,000–15,000	5,000–15,000
Phone system	500–5,000	500–5,000	500–5,000
Copy machine	800–2,000	800–4,000	800–6,500
Fax machine	1,000–3,500	1,000–3,500	1,000–3,500
File cabinets	400–800	800–1,200	1,200–1,600
Misc. furniture	1,000–2,000	2,000–3,000	3,000–4,000
Off. supplies	5,600–7,800	6,200–9,800	8,400–12,500
Displays	4,000–15,000	1,000–5,000	1,000–4,000
Warehouse Equip.			
Pallet racks		6,000–8,000	12,000–16,000
Pallets		2,000–3,000	4,000–6,000
Forklift		6,000–10,000	21,000–35,000
Conveyor		2,000–7,500	15,000–16,000
Dock board		700–1,000	1,400–2,000

Pallet jack		500–600	1,500–2,000
Lockers		700–1,000	1,000–2,000
Shelving		1,000–1,500	2,000–3,000
Work benches		500–600	1,000–1,200
Hand carts		500–700	1,000–1,500
Transportation Equip.			
Van	12,000–20,000	12,000–20,000	12,000–20,000
Truck		20,000–25,000	35,000–40,000
Leasehold Improvements			
(Gen. cont.)	30,000–60,000	15,000–30,000	22,500–45,000
Prof. Fees	1,500–4,000	1,500–4,000	1,500–4,000
Advertising	3,000–10,000	3,000–10,000	3,000–10,000
Working Capital	10,200–30,000	25,200–75,000	49,800–150,000
Inventory	2,300–49,000	23,000–122,500	57,500–490,000
Totals	82,000–230,300	149,500–393,000	282,200–939,900

Assumptions—Wholesale Businesses

1. Deposits: Rent—2 months deposit; 2,000–10,000 sq. ft.; $5–$15 / sq. ft.; Telephone—$250 / line; Utilities—$2 / sq. ft, 1–2 months security; Insurance—includes liability, fire, theft, etc.

2. Furniture & Office Equipment: Desks—$300 each; chairs—$100 each; credenzas—$500 each; bookshelves—$400 each.

3. Warehouse Equipment: Average of quotes from warehouse supply companies for new equipment.

4. Transportation Equipment: Average of quotes for vans, 16-ft. trucks ($20,000–$25,000) and 24-ft. trucks. ($35,000–$40,000).

5. Leasehold Improvements: $15–$30 / sq. ft.

6. Working Capital: 6 months rent.

7. Inventory: 23–49 percent of total assets for the following total asset ranges: no warehousing—$10,000–$100,000; light warehousing—$100,000–$250,000; heavy warehousing—$250,000–$1,000,000.

RETAIL BUSINESSES—START-UP COSTS IN DOLLARS

Type of Cost	Total Assets 10,000–100,000	Total Assets 100,000–250,000	Total Assets 250,000–500,000	Total Assets 500,000–1,000,000
Deposits				
Rent	800–15,600	1,300–31,000	2,000–33,300	3,300–66,700
Telephone	500–1,000	500–1,000	1,000–2,000	2,000–2,500
Utilities	100–200	200–300	300–400	400–800
Insurance	1,100–1,900	1,900–2,700	2,700–3,500	3,500–4,200
Furniture & Off. Equip.				
Desks, chairs	1,900–2,400	2,900–3,400	4,800–5,300	6,300–7,800
Safe	1,000–2,000	1,000–2,000	1,000–2,000	1,000–2,000
Typewriters	500–1,000	1,000–2,000	1,500–3,000	2,000–4,000
Computers	3,000–7,500	3,000–7,500	7,500–15,000	10,000–25,000
Phone system	500–3,500	1,000–3,500	3,500–5,000	5,000–7,500
Copy machine	800–2,000	1,000–3,000	1,500–4,000	2,000–3,500
Fax machine	1,000–3,500	1,000–3,500	1,000–3,500	1,000–3,500
File cabinets	400–800	800–1,600	1,600–3,200	3,200–4,400
Misc. furniture	2,000–3,000	3,000–4,000	4,000–5,000	5,000–6,000
Off. supplies	3,600–5,600	5,600–7,800	7,800–9,000	9,000–10,200
Cash register	500–2,000	1,000–4,000	1,500–6,000	2,000–8,000
Mach. & Equip.	500–13,000	5,000–32,500	12,500–65,000	25,000–130,000
Transportation Equip.				
Van	12,000–20,000	12,000–20,000	12,000–20,000	12,000–20,000
Delivery truck		20,000–25,000	35,000–40,000	55,000–65,000

Leasehold Improvements (Gen. cont.)	7,500–26,300	11,300–52,500	22,500–87,500	37,500–175,000
Prof. Fees	1,500–4,000	1,500–4,000	3,000–5,000	3,500–7,500
Advertising	5,000–10,000	10,000–15,000	15,000–20,000	20,000–25,000
Working Capital	2,400–46,800	3,800–93,700	6,000–99,900	9,900–200,100
Inventory	3,500–63,000	35,000–157,500	87,500–315,000	175,000–630,000
Totals	50,100–235,100	123,800–477,800	248,700–752,600	393,600–1,410,200

Assumptions—Retail Businesses

1. Deposits: Rent—500–1,500 sq. ft.—$10–$125 / sq. ft.; 1,500–5,000 sq. ft.—$8–$80 / sq. ft.; 2 months deposit; Telephone—$250 / line; Utilities—$2 / sq. ft.; 1–2 months deposit.
2. Furniture & Office Equipment: Desks—$300 each; chairs—$100 each; credenzas—$500 each; bookshelves—$400 each.
3. Machinery & Equipment: Represents a nationwide average of between 5 and 13 percent of total assets.
4. Transportation Equipment: Average of quotes for vans, 16-ft. trucks, and 24-ft. trucks.
5. Leasehold Improvements: $15–$35 / sq. ft.
6. Working Capital: 6 months rent.
7. Inventory: Represents a nationwide average of between 35 and 63 percent of total assets.

SERVICE BUSINESSES—START-UP COSTS IN DOLLARS

Type of Cost	Cost Range
Deposits	
Rent	3,300–11,700
Telephone	300–1,000
Utilities	300–700
Insurance, etc.	300–600
Furniture & Office Equip.	
Desk, chairs, etc.	6,300–11,400
Typewriters	500–1,200
Computers	3,000–7,500
Phone system	500–5,000
Copying machine	800–6,500
Fax machine	1,000–3,500
File cabinets	1,000–3,500
Misc. office expenses	1,000–3,000
Leasehold Improvements	
(General contractor)	15,000–60,000
Office Supplies	5,600–12,500
Professional Fees	1,500–4,000
Advertising	3,000–10,000
Working Capital	9,900–35,100
Totals	53,300–177,900

Assumptions—Service Businesses

1. Deposits: Rent—2 months deposit, 1,000–2,000 sq. ft.; $20–$35 / sq. ft.; Telephone—$250 / line; Utilities—$2 / sq. ft.; 1–2 months security.
2. Furniture & Office Equipment: Desks—$650 each; chairs—$200 each; credenzas—$800 each; bookcases—$500 each.
3. Leasehold Improvements: $15–$30 / sq. ft.
4. Office Supplies: Includes stationery, business cards, announcements, copy paper, door lettering, plants, pictures, water cooler, locks, and general office supplies.
5. Advertising: Assumes ads in local papers, telephone directories, flyers, direct mail.
6. Working Capital: 6 months rent.

average start-up costs associated with different types of businesses. These charts were prepared for me by Stewart Bauman and Alan Krasnoff, partners in the New York accounting firm of Bauman and Krasnoff, which has had a great deal of experience working with start-up businesses and entrepreneurs.

As you can see from the tables, start-up costs can be surprisingly high. It is even more surprising when you realize that the majority of small businesses are started with the personal resources of the entrepreneur. This money can be from savings, but more often than not it comes from borrowing against or selling personal assets. Banks may not lend money to a start-up business, but they will make a personal loan to an entrepreneur if it is secured by stocks, bonds, insurance policies, or real estate.

At least 50 percent of your seed capital should come from your own pocket. This will insure that you are somewhat independent of your other investors or lenders. It will also demonstrate how committed you are to the project. In fact, entrepreneurs *must* invest some of their own money in the venture. No one will rush to invest in a business if the entrepreneur doesn't show enough confidence in the idea to invest in it him- or herself. Knowledgeable investors know that if your money is tied up in the business you'll work harder and be less likely to throw in the towel when times get tough.

For many potential entrepreneurs this is the acid test. Can you risk your savings, your nest egg, your hard-earned dollars, on this venture? If the answer is no, then you aren't ready to start this business. It doesn't necessarily mean that you aren't an entrepreneur. It could mean that this is the wrong idea or that it's the wrong time for such a daring move. If you can't talk yourself into investing in the business, how will you be able to talk others into it? And it is essential to do just that, for unless you are very well off, you are going to need other people's money.

The most common sources for outside seed capital, and the first people you should approach, are your friends and relatives. They, above everyone else, should have confidence in your abilities and drive to succeed. In addition, friends and relatives are more likely than outside sources to offer lenient or flexible terms. The nest stays open in America, and there is no shame in turning to family and friends for funds, especially since they are going to profit from the business's success. Next, approach business associates. Now is the time to go after your professionals—doctors and dentists as well as lawyers and accountants. Leave no stone unturned in your search for start-up money.

But this dependence on relatives and associates can cut both ways. When a business fails it's possible for friendships to break apart and families to split into warring factions. Your decision making can be called into question and easy-going arrangements can take on the look of blood feuds. That's why it is an absolute must to frame these loan agreements in as businesslike a manner as possible, despite protests of family loyalty. Have an attorney draw up "gentle" documents— they can be in the form of a letter—indicating how the money will be paid back, when it's due, and how investors will share in profits. I'll discuss these agreements in more detail a bit later in this chapter.

Present your request for funds as an opportunity for your friends and family to share in your future profits—you are letting them in on the deal—not as a charitable contribution. If you can insure that they won't interfere in your management of the business that's great; otherwise, learn to deal with their help.

Another excellent source of seed money is a partner. Partnerships are often compared to marriages—to truly succeed they have to be based on love, not money, and you can't take them for granted.

"In partnerships everything is a potential problem," says Tim Dobel of The Tisbury Café. "I was life partners with my wife Mary Ellen before we were business partners. We knew how to balance each other and how to merge our strengths and weaknesses. I'm a good cook and know how to run the nuts and bolts of the business—cash flow, making sure we are profitable. That's not really her area. Instead, she is very good in the front of the restaurant, dealing with the public. I have to force myself to be a 'public guy.' "

Taking on a partner may also be an effective way to raise

money. Many of America's most successful small businesses began as a combination of one person who had the idea and the skill to carry it out and another person who had the cash. (In Chapter Fifteen I will discuss in great detail how to pick a partner.)

Another potential source of start-up money is a financial "angel." Angels are individuals, or groups of individuals, who put money into local enterprises. These affluent people have found that investing in small business is fun, keeps them busy, and is an excellent way to leverage their own abilities. Generally, they want to play an active role in the business, offering their services as financial experts. There are actually quite a few angels around. Your professionals may know some. Also, local governments who are actively courting new businesses may have lists of such potential investors.

Another place to look for seed capital is to your suppliers. They may offer you inventory on terms, giving you up to thirty days to pay. Consignment arrangements are not unheard of. These deals allow you to pay for only those goods that you have actually been able to sell. Rather than purchasing your equipment, you may be able to lease it with only a modest down payment. While not traditionally considered seed money, all of these supplier programs actually amount to loans.

Don't stop with these sources for seed money. There are no rules. Look anywhere and everywhere for investors. Take money from whoever offers it—as long as they are legitimate. The potential sources of start-up financing are limited only by your creativity and energy.

Before you begin beating the bushes for investors you'll have to gird yourself for the task. There are no mysteries to raising money; no slick maneuvers that guarantee you'll win people over. The only secret is knowledge.

When you approach potential investors be supremely sure of your facts. Know your business and industry inside out. Be able to answer every possible question. All the analysis and planning you've done up to this point has to be on the tip of your tongue. Questions, both factual and theoretical, have to be answered quickly, insightfully and, above all, correctly. Knowledgeable people never sound bad.

That's one reason why all of your ideas and plans should be compiled in your business plan. Not all potential seed investors will bother to read your formal plan, but it can serve as a reference and outline for you in answering questions. A business plan, as we will see in Chapter Twelve, is an outline of your idea, plans, marketing, location, customers, costs, and projections. It may be a brilliantly executed document, but it can't stand on its own. The entrepreneur has to be able to fill in the operational details—"colorize" the black and white prose—and in the process, demonstrate his or her ability to get the business off to a successful start.

It should go without saying that whether you are approaching your mother or your dentist you should be dressed well and appear alert, honest, smiling, and caring. All the traits you will bring to dealing with customers also have to be on display when you're approaching potential investors—after all, they are the first people you have to sell. Don't try to raise money when you are tired or depressed. If you've just had a fight with your spouse, reschedule the meeting. Don't combine meals with money meetings—neither party will be able to give the presentation their undivided attention. Remember that you are the ultimate expert on your business; that alone should give you the confidence you need to go out and raise money. Don't swagger, but project self-assurance. Demonstrate intelligent humility. Show the other person that you *know* your business will be a success.

Be prepared for rejection, but don't let it stop you. A "no" isn't a denial of your worth or of the validity of your idea. It may well be that your proposal doesn't fit the investor's current needs or abilities. A "no" is very often merely a reaction, not a thought-out decision.

Difficulty in raising money is not an indication of a bad idea. When I've been approached for money, whether as a venture capitalist, a banker, or just an individual investor, I've turned down lots of ideas that were later proved right. Sometimes they just didn't fit in with my own or my organization's plans. I've also loaned money for ideas that have gone sour. On average, over the years, I've agreed to lend money to or invest in one out of every thirty people who have approached me—and I'm an easy touch. Out of the businesses I've invested in only one out of every ten have actually succeeded. Obviously, my decisions to lend or not lend weren't indications of the likelihood of eventual success or failure of a business.

It is important to get used to preparing for meeting investors and coping with rejection. As an entrepreneur you will probably have to go through this process at least three times during the evolution of your business—once in search of seed financing, again for continued growth, and finally for expansion. And, if you are like most other entrepreneurs, this won't be the only business you ever start.

Before you begin looking for outside sources of seed money, you will have to decide how to treat each investment. There are two types of business financing: debt and equity. Debt financing consists of money that must be repaid—in effect, loans. Equity financing is money given to a business in exchange for some share of the ownership.

It's essential to achieve a balance between the two types of financing. If your business is highly leveraged—has a large amount of debt financing as compared to equity financing—cash flow can become a major problem because of the interest and amortization you'll have to pay. If your business is minimally leveraged—has a large amount of equity financing compared to debt financing—you won't be taking full advantage of the invested dollars. Businesses funded solely on debt financing are very risky. In fact, any loans used for seed money should be configured very carefully—with delayed repayment plans and interest accrual, if possible. Equity financing gives you some strength and protection.

Institutional investors, whom you will be approaching later on in the evolution of your business, like to see a sizable amount of equity financing as opposed to debt. Certainly, your own investment should be equity. Likewise, any money borrowed from family or partners should be subordinated debt. That means that the particular lender—a parent, for example—agrees to wait for repayment until primary or institutional lenders are paid off. This will appeal to your future, second-tier investors. They will look upon such subordinated debt as, in effect, capital in the business. If investors want some type of partial repayment, have your attorney and accountant work out a hybrid deal for them, combining aspects of both debt and equity in a convertible debenture.

As I mentioned earlier, every financing agreement you make, whether it's with a father, partner, angel, or supplier, has to be spelled out in legal form by your attorney. While each should be a custom document, they all must spell out every aspect of the agreement, including the rights and responsibilities of all parties, payment plans, maturity, interest, possible extensions, and buy-out rights. They should also include procedures for delinquency and survivorship.

Try to configure these agreements so that they take you way beyond your projected break-even point, allowing you to start paying them off out of your growing cash surplus. Never leave them open-ended or promise to pay back money sooner than you'll be able to. If you have to include a provision for early repayment, make it realistic. Try to have interest on loans accrue. That means that rather than paying it out on a regular basis, the interest simply gets added to the principal. When the loan finally does become due, pay it back over a period of years at an additional interest rate, added to the already interest-fattened principal.

Be candid in your negotiations and agreements. These agreements are for your own protection. You don't want investors to suddenly come to you and say that they need their money back for a liver transplant or any other reason.

With your seed money in one hand, pick up your business plan and cash flow with the other. Weigh them against each other. If you haven't been able to acquire the minimum your business plan calls for it's time to make a hard choice. You have three options: abandon the plan and return the money; go ahead under-capitalized; or continue your hunt for funds. If you have exhausted all your sources for seed money you can eliminate the last option. Remember: The number-one reason for the failure of small businesses is under-capitalization. Once again it comes down to your entrepreneurial personality. Are you willing to risk your money? Are you willing to risk your investors' money? The decision is yours.

CHAPTER NINE

Opening the Door

The only thing we have to fear is fear itself.
—FRANKLIN DELANO ROOSEVELT

You've begged, borrowed, and stolen enough money to meet the minimum requirements outlined in your business plan. You've driven a hard bargain with your landlord and signed a fair, or at least almost fair, lease. Experience and salesmanship have helped you line up suppliers and vendors, and your marketing plan is prepared for opening day. The only things left to do are fix up the space, hire some staff, and open the door.

In the best of all possible worlds your landlord will be paying for leasehold improvements done to your specifications. Unfortunately, not every entrepreneur is so lucky. If you are paying for your own construction work, make sure to stick to the figure you allocated in your cost projections. That can be tough since construction, regardless of how simple it is, is an expensive proposition.

Begin by carefully selecting your architect or designer (as was discussed in Chapter Four: Putting Together Your Team). He or she will be responsible for drawing up a set of plans for your space. Even if you feel comfortable with doing the design work yourself, you will still, in most cases, need a professional to initial your plans, affirming that they meet the legal codes. Don't go overboard with your plans. While a magnificent setting can be essential for a retailer, others need only a comfortable, clean, well-lighted, well-ventilated, and efficient space. Opulent surroundings can help boost your image, but they are perhaps the most expensive and least efficient means of promoting yourself. It is better to spend the money on your other marketing and promotional plans.

One retailer I know, a woman who runs a very chic store specializing in velvet clothing, accessories, and decorative arts, wanted only the best when it came to her store design. She hired a designer who thought of himself as an artist. While the results were absolutely breathtaking, the work ended up costing more than twice the original estimates and taking six months to complete.

With your designs finished and put into a formal plan, find three reputable contractors to bid. As discussed earlier, never simply hire the contractor recommended by the architect or designer. You don't want your contractor to have too cozy a relationship with the designer or architect. Either you or the person who drew up the plans must serve as a watchdog, carefully keeping an eye on the contractor. Everything from the material ordered to the hours worked must be double-checked. Similarly, your contractor should be ready, willing, and able to make suggestions about altering the architect's or designer's plans in order to save time and money. That won't happen if they have a chummy relationship.

Ask for binding bids that guarantee what your final bill will be. This may result in higher bids than if you asked for a simple estimate, but it will at least provide you with a concrete figure. Select the lowest of the three bids. Beware, however, of a bid that is dramatically (more than 15 percent) lower than the others—this could mean that the contractor is either inexperienced or a crook out to fleece you.

Have your attorney look at the contractor's contract. Make sure that it includes a firm completion date and a provision allowing you to reduce the final bill by set amounts for each day the project runs over. The contract should also stipulate that you pay in installments, holding back 10 percent of each payment so that you will have some leverage if additional work needs to be done after the project is "completed."

While your construction work is being done, start looking for a staff. I advise against simply hiring relatives—business and family may not mix. You want to be objective when it comes to employees and that might be tough if you also spend every Thanksgiving with them. Write up a brief description of the position, including salary and the experience you would like the applicant to have, and send it to the local newspaper with the biggest help wanted section. Send the same ad to the major trade magazine or journal in your industry. Contact employment agencies in your area, and try trade associations— they may have an employment service. In addition, mention to business associates and suppliers that you are looking for people. If you are looking for part-time help, contact the area high schools and colleges.

Once you have gotten responses to your ads and canvassing, cull down the applicants to the two or three you think best fill your requirements. Call each on the telephone and set up an interview.

When the candidates come to see you, immediately ask

them to fill out an application. Standard application forms that cover all the bases are available at most good office supply stores. After they have filled out the form, ask the applicants to describe their previous jobs. What have they done? What skills have they acquired? Try to find out a little about them. Ask about their interests and ambitions. Reserve judgment until the conclusion of the interview. While appearances are an important measure of a person, job interviewees are almost always nervous the first few minutes. Get an impression of the applicants. Will they work well with others? Do they seem to be honest? Conclude your interview by saying that you will contact them again when you have reached a decision.

Telephone the previous employers of each applicant. Verify what you were told in the interview and what appears on the application form. Ask how the person's performance was and how well he or she got along with people. One good question to ask is if the former employer would rehire the person if the opportunity arose.

Based on the judgments you formed through interviewing and calls to previous employers, decide who is the best person for the job. Try to weigh technical competence and personality. Both are important. If you cannot make a decision, schedule a second round of interviews, or keep looking.

OPENING DAY

The construction is completed, you've hired your staff, the shelves are stocked, your sign or shingle is hanging in front, the marketing campaign has begun, your phone is hooked up, the windows are washed, you're dressed for success, the fresh flowers are out and in bloom. Now—open the door.

Many entrepreneurs do exactly that—unlock the door one morning and wait for customers to call or come in. It's a frightening moment—one that you will never forget—perhaps the scariest day of your life. All the hard work and planning and money you were capable of mustering have gone into this one event.

But don't let your fear show. Be professional, not overly eager. Don't let those first few customers see how nervous you are—you'll only scare them off. Be upbeat, warm, and caring. And above all—smile.

If no one comes in right away don't panic. Opening a business isn't like opening a Broadway play. The reviewers can't kill you on opening night. You'll have time to make changes if they are needed. The first few weeks are when you'll have to be your bravest. Remember—you've done your homework and drawn up an accurate business plan. Give your marketing efforts some time to work. Don't blame yourself for bad weather or stock market tremors.

If no customers materialize in the first week, begin planning the next stage of your marketing program. If there's traffic, but no sales, take a second look at your inventory and pricing. In the early stages of a business it is better to be under- than over-stocked. You may not be able to purchase your products from suppliers as cheaply, but you'll gain some flexibility and safety—two vital elements for success in the first few weeks.

Some entrepreneurs try to assure a good opening-day turnout by turning it into a special event. They invite family and friends, suppliers, potential clients and customers, and members of the media to a grand opening party or sale. An opening party can be particularly beneficial to businesses whose location or business doesn't lead to a great deal of walk-in traffic. Besides providing traffic, an opening celebration can help boost your morale and calm your nerves—which by now, if you're human, are frayed.

In the past, whenever I opened a new law office I would invite family, friends, clients, peers, suppliers, and the media to a party. I used to set out fresh flowers, serve food and drink, and have some classical music playing in the background. Not only did this help soothe my nerves, it also served as added publicity and marketing. Invariably, a client remembered some matter that he or she needed to discuss with me, a peer asked for a consultation, and sometimes I'd get mentioned in the media.

If yours is a retail or service business, the first few months should be able to tell you whether or not you'll succeed. Are clients and customers coming in? Are they happy? Do they seem to be satisfied by your offerings? Encourage every satisfied client and customer to tell friends about you. If you are making sales steadily you'll probably succeed. If not, you have a problem.

Go back to your business plan and check it for possible mistakes. Redouble your marketing in general and your publicity efforts in particular. Remember that your break-even analysis predicted not only your success, but your failure as well. If, after renewed marketing efforts and fine tuning of your pricing, you still see no steady sales, jump ship. It is better to cut your losses than to pour more money into a business that has entered a death spiral. It was hard enough getting investors before you opened—when success and failure were up in the air. Think how difficult it will be to get funds for a business that has opened and isn't working.

But if you are truly an entrepreneur, if your idea passed all your testing, if you hired a good professional team, if you correctly analyzed your customer and market, if you accurately projected your costs and potential sales, if you prepared an effective marketing program, if you found a good location, and if you obtained sufficient seed money you won't have to worry too much about failure—you're going to make it.

The entrepreneurial path doesn't end here, however. Looming ahead, sooner than you may think, are a new series of obstacles. The first is your own personality.

CHAPTER TEN

The Pains of Unbundling

Perpetual devotion to what a man calls his business is only to be sustained by perpetual neglect of many other things.
—ROBERT LOUIS STEVENSON

Let's assume that you've successfully launched your business. It was a struggle at first, but you've made it. The doors are open, you have customers, and you are paying your bills. Your sales efforts have been refined and volume is reasonably predictable. Even though the opening-day excitement is gone, spirits are still running high. You may not yet have broken even, but it is clear that you are on the way to doing so. Some competitors are starting to notice you. Success seems just around the corner. Once again, you have arrived at a crossroads.

Entrepreneurial firms are like gold mines. Entrepreneurs find a product or market niche—a rich vein of ore. At first, they don't have competition. Mining the ore as fast as possible, they sell it. Suddenly, the vein of ore runs out, the same way a market dries up; or another miner begins digging close by, as competition takes notice of success. Once the ore runs out, or competition increases, there is a reduction in revenues and profit, and the costs of operating increase.

By now, the business should no longer require constant attention. It should be able to stand on its own.

Entrepreneurs, by their very nature, are preoccupied with product. Rarely do they pay attention to the day-to-day operations of the business—the infrastructure of the company. They are too busy being entrepreneurial.

But at this point, entrepreneurs must unbundle—unbundle the myriad tasks they have, so far, performed themselves and delegate them to specialists, becoming an operating manager. As a company develops, it needs more structure. You can't have mayhem in large institutions; they need order and discipline. An emerging business needs managers interested in preservation—in maintaining the process. Entrepreneurs are more interested in creation—they are project-oriented—and that can prove to be a problem.

Changing gears or delegating authority can be difficult for most entrepreneurs. They prefer to remain behind the counter, or at the work bench, rather than move into the executive suite. Unbundling is a surrender of control. Entrepreneurs, I repeat, are notoriously self-centered—they believe that no one can do a task as well as they can. Yet this self-centered approach, which was in large part responsible for their success, must be put aside.

It is essential to unbundle, since moving the business ahead will undoubtedly require more funds—for expansion, increased marketing, or new products—and that often requires more professional management. (This second tier of financing is examined in the next chapter.)

No fledgling entrepreneur is prepared for all the new tasks and responsibilities that success brings. The bundle of varied skills and traits that enabled you to reach this plateau must be broken down. Every responsibility is now magnified. One person can't handle them all—you'll need specialists. From this point on the business, rather than the entrepreneur, becomes the star. Institutional investors, or the public, lend to a business—not an individual.

Marshall Friedman of U.S. Recycling Industries unbundled, but it wasn't easy. "This company started off with two employees in addition to myself," he remembers with a certain fondness. "Since then I've had to drastically change my management style. Not only have I had to give up control of day-to-day decision making, but I've also had to delegate planning and direction to subordinates. It was frustrating at first, since I didn't realize how much of my focus would change from simply doing to organization building."

Sometimes unbundling is forced on entrepreneurs. Alan and Randy Miller of Original New York Seltzer ran a father-and-son business until Anheuser-Busch took notice of their success and approached them with a purchase in mind. "It was Anheuser-Busch's offer to buy us that inspired us to change. Even though we didn't sell out, their offer instilled discipline and business sense in us. We had to hire an attorney, an accountant, and a quality control person just to deal with them in a professional manner."

How can you shift gears and begin to unbundle? First, recognize that there are predictable stages of growth, and that your company will be like all others—it will go through the same stages. At the point where you achieve your greatest success—it is already time to change.

Second, realize that you really have to let go. In capitalism, businesses are always heading for either growth or failure. It is virtually impossible to remain the same size. Being complacent can wipe you out. Remember, it was your freshness and originality that brought customers to your business. If you try to keep things the same, you can't continue to be fresh or original.

Third, renew your commitment to the business. Many entrepreneurs are happy to rest on their laurels once their idea has been proven. It's easier to sit back and take in the applause than it is to try and top your success.

At this point you can sell the business and start over, move up to chairman and bring in professional management, or make a systematic effort to change and become a professional manager yourself.

Entrepreneurs can be categorized by the choices they make: some are "one-shot wonders"—people with one great idea and just enough drive and skill to make it happen. Having launched it, they will either become rudimentary managers or delegate just enough to keep things moving. They will be content to tread water—and maintain the status quo.

At the other end of the spectrum are the "career-entrepreneurs" who are always restless with the status quo. They thrive on instability, relish the creative process, but have an inability to keep anything going. These people will abandon the business to start something new.

In the middle of the spectrum is the "Renaissance entrepreneur"—a restless spirit who has a good idea, knows enough to get it started, and can then move toward becoming a genuine manager, or at least can surround him- or herself with the help necessary to create an organization. He or she is able to move from the short-term project orientation to the long-term process orientation that the company needs to survive.

Success puts companies in a crisis, in which growth is necessary to continue. Profitability creates a need for more funds—you'll need more employees and the resources to go after bigger markets. Growth and success will actually suck up your meager resources, often creating a cash flow crisis. As the demand for your products or services begins to exceed your company's production capacity, competitors may step in to fill the gap. Advertising will become essential, not just an option. And that will require spending at least as much as your competitors spend.

Technology costs, easily overlooked in the early stages of business, can become an important factor in the long-term survival of a company. It is essential for smaller organizations to get involved with the latest technology. To compete against established competition in larger markets requires better access to information. The big companies will already have it at their fingertips. Entrepreneurs must learn how to deal with spreadsheets, data bases, and on-line information sources, or hire people who can do it for them. Their success, up to this point, has depended largely on their quick reaction time. As the company grows, improving technology is the only way to keep reactions fast.

Charcoal Companion founder Charles Adams agrees: "As we have grown we've realized that there is more and more to learn. Without the computer we wouldn't be able to analyze the business as well. We're using it to generate all sorts of regional differences to see what works where. It saves time, allowing us to do other things."

With your business on the verge of emerging from its entrepreneurial cocoon, you'll need to bring more money into your coffers. Demand for your product or service may have outpaced your ability to purchase inventory. The time may seem perfect for expansion, either into a new product line or to an additional location. Whatever the need, it is probably not possible for you to go back to your sources of seed financing. Even if you still have some money lying around, it may not be enough for your new needs. That means it's time to go to institutional investors.

CHAPTER ELEVEN

Second-Tier Financing

A business with an income at its heels
Furnishes always oil for its own wheels.
—WILLIAM COWPER

Entrepreneurs seek second-tier financing for two different, but not mutually exclusive, reasons: to provide increased working capital to meet new needs; or to expand rapidly to assume a commanding position in their market.

First, and most commonly, businesses that have broken even, or can see that event just around the corner, often suffer cash crises. Usually, the money is coming in quickly, but there isn't enough cash on hand to replenish inventory, or to buy the equipment necessary to meet the increased demand. Since almost all businesses must pay for inventory or equipment before they receive revenue from customers or clients, they need cash on hand to pay their bills. When the business began, its capitalization—necessarily—was kept to a minimum. Now that capitalization is no longer enough. To keep up with a booming business, an entrepreneur will need more working capital.

One retailer I represent went through such a crisis last year. Her tableware and gift shop had a fabulous first Christmas season. Sales were beyond her wildest dreams. But when February rolled around she found she was in desperate need of cash. While she was waiting for her accounts receivable to come in and her inventory to shrink somewhat, she was hit with a series of bills. They were from her regular suppliers, vendors, and creditors, but they were much higher than usual, since her increased business cost more to maintain. All of her cash was tied up in her inventory. Price reductions would not be appropriate until after Easter. She was apparently in a wonderful, successful business, yet she was nearly broke.

Every type of entrepreneur faces this dilemma—not just retailers. For example, a small advertising agency may have just landed a major account. To meet the new client's demands, the agency will have to go out and buy more computers and a laser printer. Where do they get the money? They can't bill the new client yet. Or, a fledgling manufacturer convinces a major retail chain to carry its new line of toys. They need to buy more machinery—and triple production. Where do they get the money?

For most entrepreneurs, it is impossible to go back to their original investors. The entrepreneurs themselves have more than likely committed all of their net worth to get their business launched. Their friends and relatives have probably been tapped out as well. Even if some money is still available from the seed investors, it probably won't be enough to meet the new needs. The solution is to go to institutional lenders/ investors.

Working capital and small equipment needs can be met by debt financing. Since both these needs are short term, and the amounts—while too big to handle privately—are not enormous, entrepreneurs should try to borrow the money conventionally. Remember: Debt financing consists of loans that must be paid back; equity financing consists of investments made in exchange for a share in the ownership of the business. In only the most dire emergencies, and only under intolerable duress, should an entrepreneur give up equity in his or her business to meet working capital or new equipment needs. And even then I'd think twice. There may come a time when you have to give up some equity—I'll deal with that later in this chapter—but this isn't it.

SOURCES OF DEBT FINANCING

There are five main sources of debt financing: commercial banks, commercial lenders, the Small Business Administration, vendor and supplier financing, and equipment leasing. Each has its own advantages and disadvantages. In general, however, banks are the best place to start.

Commercial banks offer cheaper interest rates than any of the other sources of debt financing. The main function of commercial bank financing is to provide short-term, working capital. Banks will loan money to meet seasonal demands, to tide you over when you are between inventories, or to help you buy new equipment. Generally, banks only make loans that last one year or less. In some cases, they may make a five-year amortizing loan, but rarely do they get involved in major capital investments. The interest rates on their one-year loans will generally be slightly above the prime interest rate. Longer-term loans will carry the same interest rate as other installment loans—usually two or three points over prime.

Banks actively seek out emerging businesses. For a bank to prosper, it has to start working with a business earlier than their competitors but not *too* early in the business's life cycle for its loans to be a gamble. Bankers become interested in a business once it can show a steady, sustainable, and predictable revenue stream. They call such a business "bankable." Often, being "bankable" also means that the entrepreneur has successfully managed one down cycle.

One way to find a bank is to use your professional team—accountant and lawyer—as contacts, asking for suggestions and introductions. Consider a bank with which you already have a relationship and that services the area where your business is located. Most financial institutions prefer dealing with known quantities, and if you are a regular customer they will at least have a record of your good character and willingness to repay loans. Regional banks have been more successful than money center banks in reaching out to emerging businesses. They are rooted in the community, know the market, and know the people.

Banks are also concerned with public relations. Their business is very competitive, and anything that can boost their image in their community—such as financing Little League teams, art shows, lectures, new construction, or new local businesses such as your own—can help them attract customers.

Each bank has its own lending policy. A few phone calls can tell you how open each bank will be to your application. Ask your lawyer or accountant about the bank's reputation—do they stick by their debtors or do they cut and run? Depending on their analysis of your loan proposal—which we will get to a bit later—a bank may or may not require collateral for a loan.

Go out and actively look for banks. Work your way past junior bankers. When I was in banking, we never extended credit to a business without spending a year getting to know the principals. That can't be done today, so the lending decision is often left up to junior bankers with analytical skills but without the experience necessary to make sound judgments. You have to make sure that your banker is a truly seasoned, knowledgeable professional. Get to know the "culture" of the bank. Ask to meet the president or have coffee with the head of the corporate or commercial loan area—and use your impressions of how they treat you to get an idea of how they'd treat your business.

Commercial lenders have filled in some of the gaps created by the banks' often stodgy conservatism. If you don't match the definition of a bankable business—perhaps your financial data isn't up to banks' stringent demands—commercial lenders can be a good source of debt financing.

Generally, commercial lenders are willing to take greater risks, offer loans with longer terms, and are more flexible than banks. Many are open to creative debt-financing schemes, including floor-planning, leasing, and factoring of accounts receivable. In exchange for this flexibility, commercial finance companies charge higher interest rates than banks and have large prepayment penalties. Also, they never make loans that aren't collateralized. These trade-offs may be worthwhile for entrepreneurs unable to break down the banks' inhibitions. Many banks are affiliated with commercial lenders. If you don't qualify for a bank loan, they may steer you to a commercial lender subsidiary.

In addition to its best-known role as an information disseminator, the **Small Business Administration (SBA)** is also a source for debt financing through direct loans and fixed-asset loans, and can serve as a guarantor of bank loans to small business people.

The SBA's direct loan program is open to those business persons who have been rejected by other financial institutions (you must demonstrate at least three rejections) and functions as a court of last appeal for entrepreneurs. The interest rates are around the market average, and loans may be made for terms from five to fifteen years. The program has a reputation as a fairly easy touch, but unfortunately the waiting list is incredibly long and the paperwork extensive.

Fixed-asset loans are available from the SBA through its 503 Program, which provides long-term loans at below market rates. As with the direct loan program, 503 is designed as a last resort for entrepreneurs who have failed to find other financing for equipment, building, or other fixed-asset purchases. This program also has a long waiting list and interminable paperwork demands.

Guaranteed loans are arguably the best offerings from the SBA. The agency will guarantee 75 to 90 percent of a bank loan to a qualified small business person. Often this is just the nudge needed to get a commitment from a balky banker worried about an entrepreneur's insufficient collateral. Certain banks, because of the additional paperwork and red tape involved, won't even consider SBA-guaranteed loans, while others lower their interest rate since the federal guarantee makes the loan less risky. Still, as with other SBA programs, the paperwork is daunting and time consuming, and the process involves getting approval from two bureaucratic institutions—the SBA and the bank. That's enough to test the determination of even the most steadfast entrepreneur.

Once your business has reached the "emerging" stage, **vendors and suppliers** may become increasingly willing to offer extended payment plans—such as sixty- or ninety-day billing—or even consignment arrangements where payment is not due until the goods are sold. In effect, this cooperation is a form of short-term debt financing, and offers the entrepreneur a chance to ease some of those endemic early cash flow crises.

Many equipment suppliers offer **leasing programs,** either through their own offices or through an outside finance company, which can serve as an alternative to institutional debt financing. Most of these programs rent the equipment to the entrepreneur for a set period, applying the payments to the purchase price so that at the end of the lease period the business owns the equipment.

The advantages of such a program are many: The entrepreneur's ability to borrow other funds isn't inhibited, the terms are flexible and convenient, there is often little or no down payment, and it makes it easy to upgrade to new equipment.

PREPARING A LOAN PROPOSAL

In most cases, the entrepreneur who goes after debt financing will have to prepare a detailed loan proposal, which includes:

an up-to-date balance sheet and income statement, both pre-pared by a CPA; a pro forma budget going forward for at least the term of the proposed loan; and an executive summary—a description of the business and its management team.

Your **balance sheet** lists all the assets, liabilities, and cap-ital of your business. Assets are broken down into two cate-gories: current and long-term. A current asset is something that is readily available, such as cash, accounts receivable, or inventory. Other assets are leasehold improvements, ma-chinery, equipment, and so forth. Liabilities are also broken down into current—those that must be paid within the year—and long-term—those that are due more than a year away—categories. Capital includes your aggregate profit to date (the final number on your income statement less taxes) and any equity investments made in the business less losses.

Income statements show the current profitability of your business. The first figure in an income statement is your total sales. From this number you will subtract the costs of making those sales. The resulting number is called gross margin. Next, all other expenses—overhead costs, interest, deprecia-tion, taxes, and so forth—are subtracted from your gross mar-gin. The resulting number is your profit. Obviously, if the costs of selling and your other expenses are larger than your sales, you've suffered a loss. Income statements should be prepared quarterly. In the early stages of your business it may be wise to have them drawn up at the end of every month.

Your loan proposal should also include a comprehensive statement that will bring the lender up to date on the health of your operation.

Lenders will examine and test the relationships between various sets of numbers on your financial statements in as-sessing the health of your business. These relationships—called ratios—are good tests of the health of the business. I'll discuss their use as financial management tools in Chapter Fourteen: Financial Management.

Probably the first ratio a lender will examine is the **quick ratio**—the comparison of your most liquid current assets to your current liabilities. This is the single best indication of how healthy your business is. If current assets are greater than current liabilities the business is solvent. Lenders will closely question your accounts receivable and inventory, making sure that both are readily convertible to cash. Banks will be particularly concerned with this ratio since most of their loans are due within a year.

The next ratio lenders will look at is your **inventory turnover ratio.** This will tell them how many times a year your inventory turns over completely. Generally, the more often your inventory turns over the healthier the business and the more effective the management. There are accepted turnover ratios for every industry, and lenders will use them as a basis for comparison.

Lenders will also examine the **proprietorship ratio**—a comparison of your investment to the total assets of the business. In effect, this demonstrates how much of a stake you have in the operation. Remember, investors want to know that the entrepreneur is personally at risk.

Next, lenders will calculate your **net-net ratio**—the comparison of your net sales and net profits. This indicates the amount of profit in every sale and serves as a good measure of business efficiency. Of course, the more efficient your business, the more attractive an investor will find it.

Another way for lenders to evaluate your business (in general) and your accounts receivable (in particular) is to tabulate the **collection-period ratio.** This comparison is a bit more complicated than the others. First, lenders will divide your net sales by the total of your accounts receivable from credit sales. Then, assuming a business year of 360 days, as most investors do, they divide 360 by the number you just determined. The resulting number is the average period it takes for your business to collect its accounts receivable. A healthy collection-period ratio is one in which the period it takes to collect money from customers is only slightly longer than the period in which you must pay for your inventory.

Let's assume that after examining and testing your financial statements the lenders find your business healthy and your need for a loan legitimate. The next item they will want to examine is your **budget** or **cash flow**—a breakdown, item by item, of all the funds going out of and coming into your business month by month. I'll discuss the budget more fully in Chapter Fourteen, but for now, let's look at how a potential lender analyzes it.

It is important that your budget show the introduction of the proposed loan into your cash flow and exhibit how and when the loan will be paid back. Make sure that your budget shows that the loan will be paid back within the period required. It is suicidal to ask for a one-year loan and show in your budget that it will take two years to pay it back.

Lenders will subject your budget to a sensitivity analysis—creating a worst-case scenario to see how it will affect your ability to repay the loan. Often their sensitivity analysis involves cutting your estimated revenue in half.

If your budget survives the lenders' sensitivity analysis, they will move on to examine your statements about the qualifications of the management team, including yourself. This **executive summary** should accentuate the positive. Show your experience and how it relates to the business. Financial people are generally "number crunchers," so it's tough for them to make a loan based on character and personality. They are looking for assurances that there will be comfortable repayment of the loan. The assessment a lender makes of the quality of the management is vital. A lender's initial and continuing assessment of management is probably more important than the financial ratios, or the collateral, or anything else you can do to make your loan proposal attractive. If you have passed their financial tests and demonstrate good management, a lender may not require collateral for a loan.

To convince second-tier lenders to invest in your business you will have to show that there is a strong management team in place that doesn't depend on any one person. In other words, there must be a sound organizational structure and management succession plans—yet another reason to unbundle. Solid plans must be in place for expansion and diversification. And those plans must be outlined in the loan proposal.

In preparing a loan proposal here are some general rules you should be aware of:

- Loan proposals should be tailored to the institution receiving them. Presenting a photocopied plan telegraphs that you are shopping your company around to everyone—a signal to the investor that you are desperate or don't care enough to individualize your proposal.
- Brevity counts—no lender will read anything over ten pages. Every word counts. You must give lenders the information they need to make the deal in a clear and concise document. Get to the point of the proposal as early as possible in the document. Tell them how much you need, why you need it, and what their rewards will be—don't make them hunt for this information. Investors will spend more time examining your numbers than reading your prose.
- Don't underestimate how much money you need. These funds are going to have to carry you to the next plateau, so you'd better get enough.
- Be candid about your finances. Provide lenders with all the personal and business-related financial information they could possibly need. Show them not only that you know what they need, but that you are being up-front and honest. If you have any problems with personal guarantees or collateral, tell lenders right away. That will keep tensions down and build an atmosphere of trust.
- Even if your accountant will be at your side during meetings with potential lenders, you should be comfortable discussing the financial data in your loan proposal.
- Over-leverage is a guaranteed turn-off. Over-leverage means that there isn't enough equity already in the business. Even secured lenders want to see that at least 20 to 40 percent of your assets are covered by equity. It's the same principle used in asking for a down payment from home buyers—lenders want to see that you are putting up some of your own dollars.
- Under-capitalization also spells rejection. If your business doesn't have enough total financing to operate effectively, lenders will consider you under-capitalized and a prime candidate for failure, and therefore turn down your loan application. Incidentally, lenders often turn down loans because they are too small to make a difference in the health of the business. However, boosting your request won't suddenly

insure its acceptance, especially if your cash flow projections show that the monthly payments will be out of your reach.

• Collateral may be required. Lenders will ask for collateral if they feel at all hesitant to make the loan based on your financial data. They nearly always try to obtain collateral outside the business—a mortage on your house or a personal pledge of assets, for example. But often you can satisfy them with company collateral if it is specific enough. You may give them a lien on your accounts receivable, inventory, machinery, or equipment. Any assets put up as collateral for a loan can become the lender's property if the borrower goes into default. Lenders aren't actually looking to take possession of your collateral—they could never get true market value if they were forced to sell it. Instead, they are looking to become a lien creditor in the event of a bankruptcy. That would place them ahead of all other creditors.

LOAN AGREEMENTS

Regardless of where you find debt financing, you'll have to enter into a loan agreement. This agreement is a natural enemy of the entrepreneur. For the first time in his or her life as an entrepreneur, the borrower will have to accept outside control over his or her actions.

Traditionally, loan agreements contain two documents: a promissory note and a loan agreement. The promissory note is a simple statement that the borrower promises to pay back the loan according to the agreed terms with interest. The loan agreement, on the other hand, can be an extremely complicated document.

Conscientious lenders have to assure themselves that the borrower's business will be run rationally. Lenders also want to be immediately informed of any potential problems in the borrower's finances. In order to assure this, they write **affirmative covenants** into the loan agreement. These clauses require the borrower to take certain actions.

Most loan agreements require that the borrower supply the lender with balance sheets and income statements either monthly or quarterly, and that these be prepared by a CPA who meets their approval. These financial statements usually are required to be in comparative form, showing the present period alongside the same period from last year.

In addition, an affirmative covenant could stipulate that the borrower, or his accountant, provide the lender with a certificate representing that in the period in question there have been no financial happenings adverse to the company.

Yet another standard affirmative covenant requires the borrower to demonstrate that both he or she and the business have adequate casualty insurance. Often lenders will require the insurance company to notify them if premium bills are past due.

Other affirmative covenants may stipulate reports on the status of accounts payable—such as rent, taxes, and supplier bills—and the status of patents and licenses. I've seen loan agreements that require the borrower to maintain a predetermined net worth and profitability and to maintain certain ratios in financial statements.

Loan agreements also contain **negative covenants**—things the lender will not permit the borrower to do. Often short-term lenders will not permit the borrower to obtain other financing without notifying them and obtaining their consent. Perhaps lenders will deny the borrower the right to sign a more expensive, longer-term lease without their consent. Generally, these negative covenants attempt to restrict the borrower's right to go further into debt, thus keeping lenders safe. Restrictions may be placed on salaries and raises as well.

The longer the term of the loan, the more rigorous the covenants in the agreement. And in every case, failure to live up to an affirmative covenant or violating a negative covenant puts the loan into default, making the balance due immediately. Loan agreements can become ninety-page documents containing archaic language and provisions that defy rational explanation, all in an effort to protect the lender.

There is also a section of the loan agreement called the **events of default,** which specifies certain situations that cause the loan to come due, or mature, immediately. Standard events of default include failure to pay interest or amortization within a specified period, the termination of a lease, the loss of a patent or other valuable property, and even the death of the entrepreneur. Loan agreements often contain ten or fifteen events of default.

Obviously you'll need your attorney to take an active role in your negotiations with lenders. Never sign any loan agreements without first showing them to your attorney. Don't accept lender assertions that the agreement is standard or "boiler plate." Nearly everything in it is negotiable.

One thing that certainly can be negotiated is the frequency with which you have to deal with the affirmative covenants. It is to the entrepreneur's benefit to make the financial reports quarterly rather than monthly. At the very least this will cut down on professional fees. Wherever the agreement states that the lender's consent is required, try to add that such consent shall not be unreasonably withheld. Wherever the agreement specifies a certain number of days, try to have the number increased and defined as business days. Try to have the more onerous covenants removed to give yourself more freedom.

At the beginning of this chapter I said that there were two reasons entrepreneurs search out second-tier financing: a need for short-term working capital and an increase in capital in order to finance expansion. Debt financing is the solution for short-term working capital problems. Since the need for funds is short-term, lenders can reasonably assume that they will be repaid quickly. This affords them a great deal of safety and accounts for the large number of sources eager to work with entrepreneurs in this area.

Expansion, on the other hand, is a long-term investment. It is more than likely that the profits from such an undertaking won't appear for quite some time. That makes the investment riskier and leads the sources of this kind of funding to look for more than a simple payback with interest. They will want a piece of your business—some equity.

SOURCES OF EQUITY FINANCING

There are three main sources of equity financing for entrepreneurs: the sale of stock in the business, venture capitalists, and Small Business Investment Corporations (SBICs).

Selling stock in your company may appear very attractive, but it entails certain risks—you may have to relinquish some control over the enterprise. It's even possible to lose control of the business entirely. To sell stock, your business must be set up as a corporation. This has liability and taxation ramifications. In addition, there may be different classes of stocks. I'll discuss this fully in Chapter Thirteen: Choosing a Business Structure, but right now, let's look at stock sales simply as a means of equity financing.

Stock sales are complicated affairs, involving both federal and state laws, if the company's security (stock) sale in any way crosses state boundaries. The complications multiply as the size of the sale increases, entailing tremendous paperwork and professional fees. There are two types of stock sales: private placements, in which the stock is offered to a specific group of people only, and public offerings, in which the stock is offered to everyone.

For most emerging small businesses a private placement is the preferred method, since it does not involve as many regulations and as much expense as a public offering. In fact, any company that is incorporated, regardless of its size, can sell stock. By limiting stock sales to friends, relatives, or workers, a company can insure that shareholders will be willing to wait for long-term growth rather than demanding short-term profit.

Public offerings are difficult for small businesses to pull off since the principals have to all but guarantee a substantial return on investment. In addition, public offerings will require businesses to find a broker, or underwriter, to help sell the stock. And there are the vagaries of the stock market to worry about as well. Going public can entail new responsibilities for the entrepreneur, since he or she will now have to attend board meetings—and consider the effect any action will have on the shareholders. The entrepreneur can end up in a fiduciary relationship to thousands of strangers. There will be constant regulatory mandates to live up to as well. But the benefits can be tempting. Public offerings can raise a tremendous amount of cash, add an air of legitimacy to the company, and turn the entrepreneur into a millionaire. But public corporations also have their drawbacks.

When I was forty years old I was able to achieve my parents' wildest dream for me—I became the president of a publicly held company whose stock was traded on the American Stock Exchange. I felt I had reached the pinnacle of business success. Little did I know that I would have to become involved in the quagmire of running a public company.

It was horrendous. Not only did I have to run the business of the company, but I had to deal with the stockholders who had become my new friends, partners, and fiduciaries. I spent months and months setting up the annual meeting so that I could be sure that my board and I would be re-elected. I prayed that the stockholders in the audience would ask questions I could answer. If I had a problem with profitability I could discuss it with my wife, but not with my stockholders—they didn't want to hear about my problems. After all, they bought the stock because of the company's presumed lack of problems.

Even though stockholders may own as little as one-quarter of one percent of a company, some of them feel justified in acting as if they owned 99 percent. To them, the president of the company is their chief slave, not their chief executive. For the first time in my life I had to look at investments for their sex appeal—how they would look to the stockholders—in addition to their quality. My every move was watched. I was judged not only on my ability, but also on how I appeared. That's the kind of life you can look forward to if you go public.

Venture capitalists are in the business of investing funds in new businesses in exchange for some share in the ownership. **Small Business Investment Corporations** are venture capital companies licensed by the Small Business Administration to invest in small businesses, who obtain a percentage of their cash from the SBA itself.

Venture capitalists and SBICs always look for as much return on their investment as they can get. The average deal is a combination of debt and equity financing so that the venture capital company can sustain its internal administrative needs from the repayment of the loan, while waiting for profits from the company's growth. It's a question of risk and reward. They feel they are taking a big risk in the deal and therefore want a sizable reward.

Generally, venture capitalists will pour money into a business they believe will grow rapidly and offer substantial profits. They are more concerned with a yield on their money, and the entrepreneur's ability to deliver that return, than they are with collateral. Management is the primary factor they examine. The entrepreneur has to be flexible and knowledgeable, driven and committed.

Your timing in approaching an SBIC or venture capitalist can be crucial. Venture capitalists want to see that you've done the basic groundwork and are ready to "springboard." Your break-even point isn't as important as showing growth and potential.

As with other sources of financing it is important to know the individual preferences of the venture capitalist or SBIC you approach. Some shy away from retail and concentrate on high-tech fields, while others take the reverse approach.

When approaching venture capitalists or their representatives make sure that your attitude signals a large-scale vision for your company. These investors depend on size. They wouldn't be interested in a single dry-cleaning store, for example, unless the long-term strategic plan was to start a dry-cleaning franchise business. But don't fabricate plans—one of the entrepreneur's strengths should be his or her honesty.

While the influx of funds can be great for a fledgling business, there may come a time when the demands of the venture capitalists for return on investment threatens the life of the business. Some of the larger venture capital companies demand as high as a 30 percent return on their investment. In some cases the venture capitalist will demand that the entrepreneur buy out the investment—this is called a "put"—or the venture capitalist will sell his share of the business to another individual, corporation, or group. That can mean a sizable profit for the venture capitalist. It can also mean the demise of the entrepreneur, his or her company, or both.

DEBT OR EQUITY?

In the final analysis, second-tier financing comes down to a choice between debt and equity. Short-term needs for working capital may be followed soon by a need for increased equity for expansion. Recognizing this, many equity investors offer a hybrid arrangement in which they provide some debt financing in addition to their equity investment. This may be made part of the same deal, or the investor may lead the entrepreneur to another institution for a loan. Often, if the equity investor also provides some debt financing, he or she will allow it to become a subordinated debt.

Some form of equity financing is essential for a company to survive and flourish. With debt financing alone a business may find that all the profits from the enterprise are going to service the debt, rather than being turned back into the operation. Businesses get into a death spiral, requiring more and more debt financing to keep their operation going, yet funneling all of the increased revenues back to the lenders.

That doesn't necessarily mean that all businesses need to increase their initial equity investment. By making a substantial portion of the seed money an equity investment, entrepreneurs may be able to resist later pressures to cede some share of the ownership. Unfortunately, keeping this tight control may limit your ability to expand rapidly. It's possible that in your efforts to retain total ownership you may miss a golden opportunity to seize a larger share of market. It's possible to expand without outside equity investment, but it will take more time.

Extensive outside equity financing also has its risks. With each step in the equity financing process the entrepreneur's stake in the business goes down. You will have to strike a balance between the amount of funding you need and the amount of control you want. As time goes on the entrepreneur will find that more and more of his or her time is spent in the financial area. That's why good financial management has to be introduced into the company as early as possible.

Investors may question your choice of debt or equity financing. An entrepreneur willing to give everything—a large equity share—away will raise the eyebrows of a savvy venture capitalist. Entrepreneurs should always have a stake in the business—their being at risk shows their devotion to the deal.

BOOK II

FINE TUNING

CHAPTER TWELVE

The Anatomy of a Business Plan

Make no little plans;
they have no magic to stir men's blood.
—DANIEL HUDSON BURNHAM

A formal business plan is an essential ingredient in every business. It provides potential investors and lenders with all the information they will need to make financial decisions. While its primary role is as a money-raising tool, a business plan also serves as a map—a game plan—for your business effort, taking you from inception to success.

Drawing up a business plan forces the entrepreneur to think logically, to examine potential problems, and to make realistic assessments of future earnings. A business plan forces you to question your assumptions and ideas every step along the way. If the business is being started by a partnership, the drafting of a business plan helps bind the partners together.

I'm always amazed when I speak to entrepreneurs who have succeeded even though they never drew up a business plan. They simply winged it, and didn't do any formal projections or estimates until they had to approach outside sources of capital. In most cases they couldn't tell me when, or even if, they broke even. The risk they ran was enormous. By drawing up a business plan they could have judged the feasibility of their business rationally. They could have set minimum standards for their efforts, knowing that if they fell below them they were doomed to fail. They gambled—and won.

But I can't recommend that you follow their example. A business plan is too valuable a tool to overlook. For every entrepreneur who succeeds without a business plan there are hundreds who fail because they lack a logical, formal plan of attack. Even if you have no need for outside funding, a business plan, drawn up as early as possible and updated periodically, will be important as a means of measuring your progress.

To a large extent, the business plan can also predict the death of your business. By calculating how much seed financing you will need to start with, how much operating capital you'll need to keep open, and how much revenue you will have to bring in, you'll be able to set minimum goals. If you fall below these standards you are going to fail. The earlier you realize that your business will fail the less you will lose. Every business plan should include a danger zone that tells you when to pull up your stakes and cut your losses. This zone may change as your business and business plan evolve—that's why it is essential to update your numbers regularly.

A business plan is the company's manual, its constitution, its Bible. And like the Bible, it starts in the beginning—with the entrepreneur. (An outline of a business plan is provided on pages 173–74.)

The first page of a business plan contains the "executive summary"—a brief description of you, highlighting your strengths and competency. It should stress your technical abilities and management skills, detailing your experience. Don't underestimate the importance of this brief self-description.

When I was a venture capitalist I received hundreds of business plans a month. The first thing I did was read the executive summary. If it didn't hook me I rejected the plan without reading any further. Investors and lenders are unanimous in citing the personal integrity and strength of management as prime factors in their decision to jump in or stay away. Why are you the right person to start and run this business? What skills do you possess that make it likely that you will succeed? Corny as it may sound, traditionalism is a virtue—tried and true values such as good character, business morality, and a willingness to work hard are traits that potential investors believe in and look for.

The next section of your business plan spells out the purpose of the business—a crystallization of your idea in writing, paying particular attention to what sets you apart from everyone else. The key here is to answer the question: What business am I in?

Describe the marketplace you are entering. Discuss the general trends in the industry, and gradually narrow your description to include the segment of the market you are going after, and then the specific niche you are targeting.

Keeping your analysis of your trading area in mind, define the geographical limits of your market.

Describe your target customer, whether it's an individual consumer or another business. Customers should be described in terms of age range, income range, sex, education level, and interests. Note the size and decision-making pattern of any markets you are targeting.

Analyze why the target customer buys the particular product or service, taking into account all of their motivations.

Describe your product or service in detail, touching on how you will make it, how you will purchase it, or how you will provide it. Fully analyze how much it will cost you to make it, purchase it, or provide it, and explain your sources of supply, the quality of their materials, and the relationship you will have with them. Touch on any potential problems in procuring or dispensing your product or service. Will it become obsolete or go out of fashion quickly? If so, describe how you will react to changes in the market, and how quickly you can implement these reactions.

You must also address your competition. Describe how many competitors there are, what market segments they serve, how well they are doing, and how you will stack up against them. Present any data that you have been able to gather on their sales and market shares. Make sure to document fully the advantages and disadvantages you will have in competing with each.

The next step in the business plan is to describe your marketing plan, explaining exactly how you will convince customers to buy your product or service rather than that offered by the competition. Explain how you will encourage sales through advertising, promotion, and public relations. Analyze and document how much this will cost. Make sure you offer clear-cut strategies for reaching your goals.

Note how much the product or service is worth to the customer, what the competition charges, and at what price you can make the most profit. Break down your distribution pattern—how you will dispense the product or service to the customer. In the case of a retail store, describe the type of location you need.

Now comes the hardest part—the financial breakdown of your business. Itemize every single start-up cost for the business from rent and space renovations to insurance and advertising. Make sure that you touch on every possible cost. Describe how much equity financing you will be providing, and how much additional equity and debt financing will be necessary. Note likely payback rates for your loans and plans for returning profit to the sources of your equity financing. Using your start-up cost estimates and your proposed financing, compile an opening-day balance sheet. Then extend your financial section by preparing projected income statements for your first three years in business, and a cash flow statement for your first year. Explain when you expect to break even.

When preparing your financial projections, make sure your assumptions will stand up. If you are projecting revenue to increase each year for three years, show what you are basing this on—increased sales, greater market share, or higher prices. Investors and lenders will try to tear your assumptions to shreds, substituting their own projections based on worst-case scenarios. You have to be able to back up your projections. Investors look at your projections as an indication of your thoughtfulness, thoroughness, and honesty.

Remember that you are trying to entice outside capital. This financial information is an absolute requirement for investors, and the greater the detail you offer the better. Mapping out one year isn't enough—go forward at least three years. For the first year, make monthly projections. For the second year, make quarterly projections. The third year can be treated annually.

Briefly explain the legal structure of your business, any licenses you will need, and potential regulatory and zoning problems.

If you have professional help lined up—an accountant, attorney, architect, or contractor—describe their qualifications. How many employees will you need and what will they do? If they are experienced, stress that fact. Remember, you will be calculating professional fees and employee salaries for your financial statements, so there is no reason not to tout the benefits they bring to your business. Suggest your ability to manage as well as create.

Your business plan should, of course, be typed, and if possible, be bound. Its appearance is a reflection of your seriousness. This document will represent you to potential investors ranging from friends and family to bankers and venture capitalists—it should be done as clearly, concisely, and professionally as possible. Don't make the plan too long—investors won't want to read it. Try to keep it as lively as possible. If your business involves the selling, distributing, or manufacturing of a product that is special in any way, send a sample of the product along with the plan. If you don't have samples, send photographs. In fact, relevant photos and graphics can be a big help. Logo designs, floor plans for stores or other facilities, photos and descriptions of specialized equipment can all help. But avoid being too flashy.

Try to make each business plan a custom package. I was always turned off by business plans that were numbered or generic—I didn't want to be competing with other lenders. With today's word processing and desktop publishing technology, it should be possible to personalize each business plan submitted.

Along with any business plan submitted to a potential investor, include a simple cover letter stressing your abilities and detailing how much of an investment you are looking for.

Sophisticated people immediately jump to certain parts of the business plan. Most do as I used to, and read the executive summary first, trying to determine exactly what kind of person the entrepreneur really is. Next, people will read information about your industry. Is it interesting? Does it offer growth potential? After that, most look into the planned location. Does it fit the type of business being planned? Is the area economically healthy? What are the demographics of the community? If the savvy potential investor is satisfied with those three issues, he or she will move on to the financial projections. Smart investors won't look so much at profitability—every business plan, after all, predicts success—but at how the figures are put together. Do they show intelligence and financial acumen? Finally, the investor will look at their payoff—what's in it for them.

It can take months of full-time research and writing to prepare a business plan. Some entrepreneurs try to speed up the process by hiring outside services to prepare the plan. Fees for this type of work can run from two thousand to ten thousand dollars. Regardless of how much or how little it costs, and how much time it may save, I strongly advise against letting an outsider draw up your business plan. The

BUSINESS PLAN OUTLINE

1. Executive Summary (a condensation of the entire plan)
   a. State the mission of your business
   b. Briefly describe your product or service
   c. Touch on your marketing strategy
   d. Present your revenue projections and future plans
   e. Explain the structure of the business
   f. Provide sketches of your management team
2. Business Description
   a. Explain, in detail, your particular product or service
   b. Describe how your customers will obtain the product or service
   c. Show how your product or service meets customers' needs
3. Market Analysis
   a. Using demographics, define your target customers
   b. Explain why this customer will buy your product or service
   c. Discuss the potential size of the market
   d. Define economic and social factors that influence the market
   e. Identify any significant industry trends
   f. Discuss competitors and how you relate to them
4. Finances
   a. State how much equity financing you will be providing
   b. Indicate how much additional debt and equity financing you'll need
   c. Provide a projected income statement for three years.
      • break the first year down month by month
      • break the second year down by quarters
      • treat the third year annually
      • state the assumptions used to prepare the projections

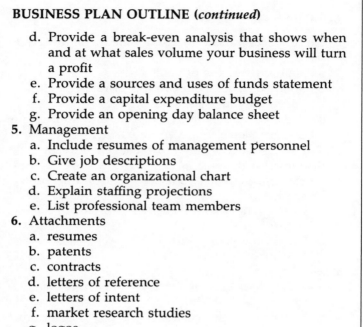

BUSINESS PLAN OUTLINE (*continued*)

    d. Provide a break-even analysis that shows when and at what sales volume your business will turn a profit

    e. Provide a sources and uses of funds statement

    f. Provide a capital expenditure budget

    g. Provide an opening day balance sheet

5. Management

    a. Include resumes of management personnel

    b. Give job descriptions

    c. Create an organizational chart

    d. Explain staffing projections

    e. List professional team members

6. Attachments

    a. resumes

    b. patents

    c. contracts

    d. letters of reference

    e. letters of intent

    f. market research studies

    g. logos

    h. designs

blood, sweat, toil, and tears you put into the drafting of your own business plan will be repaid a hundredfold by the knowledge you acquire.

Some excellent sources for more advice on writing business plans, and even sample plans to look over, are *Starting and Managing the Small Business,* by Arthur H. Kuriloff and John M. Hemphill, Jr. (McGraw-Hill); *How to Prepare and Present a Business Plan,* by Joseph R. Mancuso (Prentice-Hall Press); the Small Business Administration, which publishes a series of brochures and pamphlets; and large accounting firms, such as Ernst & Whinney, which have offices all around the country and publish guides and booklets on business issues.

CHAPTER THIRTEEN

Choosing a Business Structure

Form ever follows function.
—LOUIS HENRI SULLIVAN

As soon as you decide to go into business speak to your accountant and attorney to determine the best legal structure for your company. Most entrepreneurs have three options: sole proprietorship, partnership, or corporation. Your choice of business structure should be made with two things in mind: liability and taxation. In addition, your selection of a business form may affect your chances of getting financing.

Sole proprietorships are generally businesses that are organized and operated by a single individual. Simplicity is one advantage of starting as a sole proprietorship. The accounting and legal work that goes into the formation and maintenance of a sole proprietorship is the lowest of any of the forms. Also, sole proprietorships pay the lowest taxes.

However, there are disadvantages to the form—primarily liability. The sole proprietor is personally liable for every debt and obligation of the business. Today, the environment for liability suits—particularly cases involving product liability— is overheated. The market for commercial liability insurance is skyrocketing—and the prices are astronomical. Sole proprietorship is a good option only if you can afford adequate insurance.

Other disadvantages of the sole proprietorship form may appear later in the life of the business. Most sole proprietorships don't have the capital resources to expand. You'll have only your personal credit and assets to draw against. Stock can only be sold by a corporation. And with only one person there is obviously limited expertise to be drawn on. Finally, the personal and business finances of a sole proprietor are forever inexorably intertwined. The business can never really take on a life of its own.

The second option is a partnership—a business that is organized and operated by two or more individuals. From a tax point of view partnerships are identical to sole proprietorships. All income and expense items pass through to the partners. There are extremely important differences regarding liability, though.

In a partnership, you will be liable for all the obligations that your partner or partners incur in the course of operating the business. You'd better trust them. On the other hand, creditors of an individual partner cannot come after property owned by the partnership. They can only attach the interest and income of the individual partner.

Partnerships have some of the same disadvantages as sole proprietorships, and may also place an emotional burden on the entrepreneur. When you have a partner or partners, you will have to immerse yourself in organizational psychology. Decisions are no longer determined by what is best for you, but by what is best for the organization. And that will be determined by two or more people. This could easily lead to personal conflicts. I'll discuss partnerships in greater detail in Chapter Fifteen: How to Pick a Partner.

, Incorporation is the third option for entrepreneurs. A corporation is an artificial being created by law. A corporation is formed by applying to the secretary of state of whichever state will be the legal home of the corporation. The choice of which state to incorporate in is, in itself, an important decision, since corporate laws, taxes, and regulations vary. The secretary of state will then issue a charter—the license that enables you to operate and form the corporation, stating simply that you are incorporated.

The owners of a corporation are its stockholders. The money paid by stockholders in exchange for stock becomes the capital of the corporation. The stockholders are *not* responsible for any of the debts of the corporation. Their only liability is the money that they have invested to get their stock or loans they may have made to the corporation.

Incidentally, this loaning of money to the corporation is a standard ploy used by many entrepreneurs. Equity investments may yield profits that will be subject to taxes. Loans, on the other hand, are paid back and don't necessarily become taxable. Entrepreneurs, eager to get back their initial investment without paying taxes on it, try to configure much of it as loans to the corporation. Banks—and the Internal Revenue Service—don't take kindly to this type of arrangement, which is called a "thinly capitalized" corporation. In fact, the IRS limits the amount of investment in a corporation that can be structured as loans.

Most small businesses form what are called closely held corporations—which means that the stock is owned entirely by a few private individuals, and is not traded on any securities exchange. Some states have two different sets of corporate laws and regulations: one dealing with closely held corporations, the other with larger corporations.

A corporation is run by its board of directors, who are chosen by the stockholders and are responsible for the large-scale decision making. The board, in turn, chooses officers—president, vice-president, secretary, and treasurer—who are responsible for the day-to-day operations of the corporation.

The corporate structure has many advantages. The main reason entrepreneurs choose to go into business as a corporation is to take advantage of the limited liability it affords them. The corporation is considered a being. It has its own liability to the extent that it has money in the bank and assets. When someone sues a corporation, he or she sues the corporation itself, not the stockholders. Since there is no physical corporation to serve with legal papers, most states stipulate that offices of the secretary of state may accept a summons for you.

Another advantage of the corporate structure is that it has perpetual existence. Stockholders can die, but the corporation doesn't. Stock becomes part of an individual's estate and can be passed on to heirs.

Corporations can raise money by selling additional stock to investors. Even though stockholders are theoretically owners of the corporation, that doesn't mean they have a role in running the business. The stockholders' only real power is in voting for board members once a year at an annual meeting. By keeping the majority of voting power in the hands of friendly stockholders—such as family and friends—an entrepreneur can insure that he or she will be in command, while continuing to raise money.

I recommend that if you form a corporation, you draw up an agreement among all the stockholders. This agreement should address potential problem areas. For example: Who will be running the corporation? An agreement can provide for management control by the entrepreneur and state who the officers of the corporation will be. What happens to the stock when a stockholder dies? Very often, stockholder agreements will call for the shares to be sold back to the corporation rather than pass on to an estate. Perhaps you don't want your stockholder's children to become involved in your business. What happens if stockholders want to sell their stock? You may not want strangers to come into your corporation. The agreement can require that such stock be offered to the other stockholders at a predetermined price. Stock purchase plans, funded by insurance policies, can be drawn up to take care of these situations.

The corporate structure allows for a great deal of fundraising flexibility. You can create different classes of stock for different types of investor personalities. Let's look at an example. A share of preferred stock in your corporation may be targeted to conservative investors, like family members. In the event the corporation is liquidated, they are first in line to be paid—right after creditors, and before holders of common stock—making the investment relatively safe. Preferred stock could also have a small dividend attached. A share of common stock in your corporation could be targeted to more adventurous investors. Holders of common stock might be entitled to divide all the profits left after the preferred stockholders get their dividend. In a good year, common stockholders would do much better than the preferred stockholders. In an off year, the preferred stockholders are at least guaranteed a dividend. You can have as many classes of stock as your imagination and ingenuity allow, each designed to fit different investors.

Some third parties are impressed by the corporate structure, thinking that it lends an air of formality and seriousness, thus making the venture less risky. But don't think that incorporating will keep you from having to personally guarantee loans. The corporate structure can rarely be used as a shield from sophisticated lenders or creditors. They are aware of the device and will require personal guarantees from the stockholders of the corporation. In addition, they may send two sets of bills—one to the corporation and another to a major stockholder.

I believe that entrepreneurs who will be leasing commercial space should always form a corporation—even if it is for the sole purpose of signing the lease. You can do business using whatever structure you desire, but by having a corporation sign the lease you limit your liability. If you must break the lease the landlord will only be able to go after the corporate assets. A landlord accepting this technique, however, will probably require more substantial deposits than otherwise.

In addition, there may be some marketing advantages to being incorporated. If your customers prefer to do business with corporations, you had better be a corporation. Many service businesses incorporate simply to look important.

The main disadvantage to the corporate structure is that the tax rates are much higher than for sole proprietorships or partnerships—and corporate profits can be subject to double taxation. That is, the stockholders of a corporation have to pay income taxes on dividends they receive on their shares. The corporation itself must pay a tax on profits before it can become dividends.

For example: A corporation must pay taxes of, let's say, 28 percent on $100,000 in profits. That reduces the profit to $72,000. This is passed out to shareholders in the form of a dividend. If there were ten shares of stock, each would receive a $7,200 dividend. The shareholders now must pay personal income tax on their dividends. Of course, if the shareholders receive a salary from the corporation, they will have to pay income tax on that as well.

One possible way around this double taxation is to form a Subchapter S Corporation. This refers to a tax category in the IRS code. In a Subchapter S Corporation, income or losses are passed through directly to the shareholders, based on their percentage of ownership. But while the federal government recognizes this right of Subchapter S Corporations, not every state or city goes along with it. It's possible that, on the state level, the added cost of double taxation could offset the benefits of the Subchapter S structure. That's why you need an experienced accountant and attorney to evaluate your options.

Accounting and legal fees vary depending on the business structure chosen. A good rule of thumb is that sole proprietorships will pay the lowest fees, partnerships will pay a bit more, and corporations will pay the most.

Your choice of a business structure will have its greatest effect during the unbundling stage. The decision you made in structuring the business will determine what you can and cannot do. However, choosing one structure in the early days of the business doesn't keep you from changing to another form later on. But for simplicity's sake you should start as a sole proprietorship or partnership and then become a corporation, contributing your assets to the organization. It can be more difficult to go from a corporation to a sole proprietorship or partnership. Once you put your eggs in a corporate basket, taking them out will cost you money. Liquidation may require you to declare sizable dividends to shareholders, who will have to pay taxes on the income. In addition, the liquidation itself could require the corporation to pay taxes.

CHAPTER FOURTEEN

Financial Management

Money alone sets all the world in motion.
—PUBLILIUS SYRUS

Not all successful businesses proceed according to plan. Even well-researched and documented business plans can be off the mark. In fact, most of the entrepreneurs I have interviewed, counseled, or made loans to admitted that their projections were a bit off. Usually, the ever-optimistic entrepreneurs over-estimated their sales, under-estimated their costs, and failed to break even as early as they projected.

Most fledgling entrepreneurs believe that the surest sign of success is the ringing of the cash registers. Nothing could be further from the truth. Sales and profits are not the most accurate ways to measure the health of a business. The entrepreneur who gauges his or her business by its sales and profits is like the doctor who looks at a patient's appearance, feels that the skin is warm, and pronounces him or her healthy. There is much of importance below the surface, under the skin of a business.

I've seen retail stores die suddenly. One day the store is packed with shoppers, the shelves are brimming with merchandise, the stock room is filled to the rafters, and there's a line at the cash register. The next day the doors are closed and there's a "Gone Out of Business" sign in the window. How is that possible?

Lurking under the surface of every business are the factors of break-even, cash availability, and inventory liquidity. Combined, these make up the real pulse of a business. Certainly, sales are vital. But on their own, without sound financial management—the control of those three factors—they cannot keep a business alive. To gauge the health of your business you will have to understand balance sheets and income statements—two tools I discussed earlier in the book—as well as the financial implications of pricing, cash flow, and financial ratios.

Pricing and Cash Flow Analysis

There is probably nothing more perplexing than setting a price for goods or services. Usually gregarious business persons clam up when asked about how they determine their prices. In some industries pricing may be uniform. The easiest way to set a price is to simply charge what everyone else does, and then try to increase volume or cut costs. Unfortunately, not all entrepreneurs have it that easy. Perhaps you are selling a unique product or service. In that case, you will have to do some financial analysis.

Begin by examining your costs. There are two types of costs of doing business: variable costs and fixed costs. Variable costs are those that vary directly with sales—as sales go up these costs go up, and as sales go down, these costs go down. A good example would be the cost of the wood needed to make hand-made toys. The more toys you sell, the more wood you have to buy. Variable costs can include raw materials, packaging, and sales commissions.

Fixed costs are those that do not change as sales increase or decrease. No matter how many toys you sell, for example, your rent is unaffected. Most entrepreneurs are amazed at all the fixed costs they will be faced with: rent, salaries, fees, advertising, promotion, taxes of every shape and kind, water, electricity, insurance, window cleaning, exterminating, garbage collection, telephone, cleaning and maintenance, professional dues, continuing education, upkeep of business libraries, credit card fees, and inventory. And this list just scratches the surface.

Some of the best sources for estimates of the variable and fixed costs of different businesses are other small businesses. If you are going to be opening a hand-made toy store in Baton Rouge, contact the operator of a similar store somewhere else. Generally, business people will be willing to pass along such data to non-competitors. Trade associations can be great sources for costs—they usually have data on the average costs of their members.

Your local utilities should be able to provide you with estimates of electricity, gas, water, and telephone charges. Suppliers can help in estimating how much you will need to spend on equipment upkeep and inventory. Neighboring businesses will know what cleaning, garbage, and exterminating costs are. Credit card fees are generally 2 to 15 percent of sales off the top.

Figuring out how much you will be paying in taxes can be an exercise in terror. You may have to pay a commercial rent tax; a portion of your landlord's real estate tax; federal, state, and local income tax on either a personal or business return; maybe even an unincorporated business tax (New York City's can amount to 4 percent of your net income). There is also payroll tax, which is an amount equal to what is withheld from employees' checks for Social Security. Don't forget unemployment insurance, which can amount to $300 per year per employee to the state, and another $60 per year per employee to the federal government. If you are going to offer medical insurance for your employees, that can run as high as $2,500 per year per employee.

Here's where accountants really earn their fee. They will have to be able to navigate through all of this information and provide you with an accurate guide to how much you will be paying each month. In fact, a good accountant should be able to work out a series of different scenarios for you, depending on which business structure you choose, how much, if anything, you take in salary, and other decisions you make.

Make a rough estimate of your pricing, based on your planned marketing and promotional program. Ask yourself a series of questions about your business:

- Is your product or service unique enough to command a high price?
- Are there any legal limits on how much you can charge?
- How will competitors respond to your pricing?
- Are there market conditions—such as new technology, pending legislation, or new sources of supply—that could affect your price?
- Will you have to work through middlemen to get your product or service to the public? If so, what is their pricing policy?

Using this information, you can project forward and see what level sales have to reach for you to break even. If the estimated sales price of your toys is $3, and your variable costs are $1, the $2 left over is called the contribution margin. Let's assume that the fixed costs of your toy business are $10,000 monthly. By dividing the fixed costs of $10,000 by the contribution margin of $2, you discover that to break even you will have to sell 5,000 toys each month.

Another thing to look at is your markup. Markup is the

difference between your selling price and purchase cost. It is generally considered as a percentage rather than as a dollar amount. If you are buying men's shirts from a vendor for $10 and selling them in your store for $15 your markup is 50 percent. If you sell the shirts for $20, your markup is 100 percent. There are accepted industry-wide markups, which can be obtained from trade associations. But even with these as a guideline you will still have to make an independent decision. Remember that price is also a marketing tool. A higher price, and therefore, a higher markup, may imply high quality and exceptional service.

Pricing is a difficult thing to decide upon. Many factors, from finance to marketing, come into play. The best advice I can offer is a word of caution: It is always easier to lower prices than it is to raise them. Aim high and hope for the best. If you find yourself in trouble, aim a little lower.

THE SIGNIFICANCE OF CASH

One of the biggest problems business people face is cash flow. Without cash on hand a business will die, however high its sales or profitability. Cash is the blood of a business. It moves in and out of a business with incredible speed. It comes in when customers pay their bills. It moves out when the entrepreneur pays his or her bills. Simply put, cash flow is the difference between what you take in and what you pay out. If a business pays out more than it takes in it will, obviously, be short of cash.

Remember, cash doesn't necessarily come in when a customer makes a purchase or go out when you place an order. Since few businesses are run on a totally cash and carry or cash on delivery basis terms become vital. Many customers and clients will want to pay for goods or services some time after they actually acquire them, through some sort of credit buying. Similarly, you, as a business person, will want to pay your suppliers, staff, and creditors some time after you acquire goods or services from them. The trick, of course, is to take in cash from your customers or clients before you have to pay your own bills.

The simplest of all businesses is one in which every sale

made is a cash transaction, all bills are paid in cash at the end of the day, and there is no remaining inventory. An entrepreneur would take the money out of the cash register after the day's last sale, pay the staff, purchase supplies, goods, or raw materials for the next day, pay all expenses incurred on that day—rent, taxes, utilities, and so forth—and pocket the surplus. This simple model just doesn't exist, however. Service businesses do come close to it—that's another reason for their growing popularity. But even in the best service businesses, customers and clients will often pay on terms, forcing the business person to also pay on terms.

A successful business person will therefore have to be able to forecast and analyze the cash flow of his or her business. You'll want to know if there is a big bill looming on the horizon, or if sales are about to slow down. Cash flow analysis can give you the time needed to tackle problems. That's important, since it may require months to get short-term loans to cover your seasonal ups and downs. You don't want to close shop on Friday and suddenly realize that you won't be able to pay your bills on Monday. That's when businesses suffer "the cash flow heart attack"—an otherwise healthy-looking operation suddenly, without warning, keeling over dead. But, of course, as with heart attacks, there are warning signs if you know what to look for. That's where cash flow analysis comes in.

Begin by projecting your income month by month. Then subtract from each month's income what it will cost you to keep the business up and running. These numbers will have to be estimates in the beginning, but as time moves on you can replace them with actual numbers. These estimates come from the market research you did when calculating how much seed money you would need to start the business. Your projections will have to be based on a series of assumptions. Not only are you assuming that your sales will be a certain amount, but you must also assume customer payment terms, supplier payment terms, loan or investment payback terms, and any re-investment of cash in the business—digging into your own pocket to account for cash shortages. Work forward three years, or until you can show that the business will break even.

This cash flow analysis will be a vital part of your business plan. Potential investors will scrutinize it carefully, looking for potential problems and invalid assumptions. It will also be the single best way for the entrepreneur to track the true health of his or her business. Income statements don't take into account the terms of transactions. They simply list sales as income. That's fine if you are offering no credit or terms to your customers. But since most businesses are forced to offer some type of term arrangement, income doesn't really reflect how the business is doing. It's entirely possible to show a profit on your income statement and actually be short of cash.

In order to continue using cash flows as a gauge of business health you will have to keep accurate records of all of your finances. I can think of no better use for a computer than as a way to keep, compute, and analyze cash flow. This study of your financial track record is absolutely vital to good financial management. And as I'm sure you realize by now, good financial management is a necessity for success in business.

Develop an effective cash management system. Your goal is to collect checks written to you as quickly as possible, while delaying clearing checks you write to others as long as possible.

In order to collect checks written to you quickly, take advantage of the latest banking technology. You can establish decentralized collection points at banks all over the country, and then have the funds wired electronically to your own local bank. This will let you use your funds more quickly.

The period between the time you write a check and the time the funds actually leave your account is called the "float." One unusual way to lengthen your float without jeopardizing your credit standing is to open a bank account on the opposite end of the country and pay bills from that account. This could give you up to ten extra days of float.

RATIO ANALYSIS

Another good method for analyzing the financial health of your business is to keep an eye on the relationships, or ratios, of certain sets of numbers that appear on your balance sheet and income statement. These ratios actually tell you more about the business than the statements themselves. All of these ratios can be used to analyze a business yearly, monthly, weekly, or even daily.

The first ratio to be aware of is the comparison of your **current assets to current liabilities,** both of which are noted on your income statement. This current ratio not only indicates financial health, but also determines how much working capital you have available. Let's say that your business has $20,000 in current assets and $10,000 in current liabilities. That means your current ratio is 2:1. It also means that you have $10,000 in working capital—the difference between your current assets and liabilities—to take care of expenses other than your current bills. A current ratio of 2:1 is considered standard and safe. It gives you some room to take care of emergencies and allows for some inventory spoilage and theft (known in business jargon as "shrinkage"). But there may be cases when another current ratio is preferable. If your market is a stable one in which there is little change due to season, style, or technology, you can probably get by with a lower current ratio, perhaps 1.5:1. On the other hand, if you are carrying a great deal of debt that may come due at anytime, a higher current ratio, in the range of 3:1, may be in order. Check with comparable successful businesses and trade associations for the industry norm.

A slight variation on the current ratio is the **quick ratio.** This is the relationship between your quick assets—those that can instantly be turned into cash—and your current liabilities. These assets would *not* include your inventory. For example, out of your $20,000 worth of current assets you have quick assets of $15,000. Compared with your current liabilities of $10,000, this gives you a quick ratio of 1.5:1. This is an excellent ratio to look at when examining worst-case scenarios. If, for some reason, all your current liabilities come due at once, you should be able to pay them. With a quick ratio of 1.5:1 you would be able to deal with such a crisis and still have a safety margin. Try to keep a quick ratio of at least 1:1. Any lower and you are flirting with disaster.

Another important ratio to consider when working out your cash flow is the **collection-period ratio.** This will indicate how long your cash is being tied up in customer or client credit. The sooner you receive cash from your sales, obviously, the better off you are. This ratio is a bit more complicated to figure out. Let's say your business has net sales of $250,000 and accounts receivable from credit sales of $25,000. By dividing your net sales ($250,000) by your accounts receivable ($25,000) you come up with a result of 10. Most financial analysts assume, for simplicity's sake, that there are 360, not 365 days in a year. Divide 360 days by the result of your earlier arithmetic—in this case, 10. The result is 36, meaning that, on average, your credit customers are paying their bills within 36 days.

Now, to see how efficient your credit sales are, you will have to compare this period of time to the terms you receive from your suppliers. For example, the standard policy of most suppliers is to require payment in full within 30 days of delivery. By subtracting the terms you receive from your suppliers (30 days) from the time in which your customers are paying their bills (36 days), you can gauge the effectiveness of your credit policy. In general, a business is considered healthy when this number is no more than 15 days. If it is less than 10, as in our example, you are running a very efficient operation. Of course, the policies and practices of your particular industry should be used rather than generalities.

You can see from this ratio how important the terms you get from your suppliers are. Many small businesses fail simply because they bought under harsh terms. While the quality of your vendor's product is important in being able to sell it, the terms you buy under are equally important. A good relationship with a vendor can be the difference between success and failure for a new business. Once a vendor cuts back on terms, requiring you to pay cash on delivery, it can send your business into a death spiral. You'll have to stop offering customer credit and run your own business on cash on delivery terms. That's doom in today's credit-driven economy.

Other ratios help determine how profitable a business is. One such comparison is the **return on equity ratio,** which examines the relationship between the business's profit and the amount of money invested. This is calculated by dividing the entrepreneur's equity or net worth by the company's net income.

A more accurate way of calculating profitability may be to work up an **entrepreneurial return on equity ratio.** This takes into account the value of fringe benefits and the salary that an entrepreneur may have sacrificed by not taking a regular job. It is calculated by adding the value of the entrepreneur's pay and perquisites to the company's net income, subtracting any sacrificed salary, and then dividing the entrepreneur's equity or net worth by the result.

Another way of gauging profitability is to determine the **return on sales ratio.** This compares profit with sales volume, indicating whether the company is getting an adequate profit on its sales. To arrive at this figure, divide net sales by net income.

If any of these profitability ratios are lower than industry norms, the entrepreneur should try to discover why. Perhaps expenses need to be cut or sales need to be increased. If profits have been reinvested in unproductive assets, these assets should be liquidated as soon as possible. Maybe the company is under-leveraged. In that case, the entrepreneur should consider getting additional loans to allow him or her to withdraw more money.

One final ratio that can be helpful to entrepreneurs is the **debt to equity ratio,** which compares a company's liabilities to its equity. It is calculated simply by dividing total equity by total liabilities. Too high a figure means the business is over-leveraged. If that's the case, entrepreneurs should try to reduce their debt, improve profitability, and reinvest profits in the business.

Ratios are excellent tools, but they do have some limitations. First, your ratio analysis is only as reliable as the data you base it on. Remember the old computer programming adage: garbage in, garbage out. Second, since ratios are only valid as comparisons, make sure that you are comparing numbers that reflect the same period of time. Comparing monthly sales to yearly costs, or vice versa, is worthless. Third, ratio results may mean different things in different businesses. For example, a high inventory turnover ratio may indicate a shortage of goods and a poor stocking of inventory. Yet it could also suggest a very good sales and inventory control system. Be careful to determine the true nature of your findings.

INVENTORY LIQUIDITY

Cash flow problems often develop when business people are forced to stock inventory. When you buy material from a supplier you are committed to paying for it, in cash, by a certain time. At the point when you pay your supplier you will not, in all probability, have sold all your inventory. That means you have cash tied up in inventory. Remember, this cash actually loses its value. First, the inventory itself becomes less and less valuable as time goes on. The longer it sits unsold the more likely it will spoil, become obsolete, or have to be sold for a lower markup. Second, cash tied up in inventory could have been used elsewhere. The one hundred dollars it cost you to buy stock could have been put into the bank where it would have earned interest. It also could have been put to use paying another bill. This is called the opportunity cost of money.

The smaller your inventory, the better off you are. Of course, you have to have enough supply on hand to meet your customers' demand, but having any more than that costs you money. In the early stages of a business it's extremely difficult to make inventory decisions. You have no real assurances that sales will meet your projections. That's why you have to do adequate research about comparable businesses. Here's one more instance where experience in a business or industry pays off. The best advice I can give you, other than doing your homework, is to buy lean. It is better for a new business to run out of an item and lose a sale than to overstock and tie up your rarest possession—cash—in inventory.

Besides relying on experience, entrepreneurs can calculate yet another ratio to judge the quality and value of their inventory. Calculating the **stock to sales ratio** will tell you how many times a year your inventory will turn over completely. First, determine your average inventory. Let's say that your year-end inventory is $25,000. Next, divide your net sales for the year—$100,000—by your inventory figure—$25,000. The result, four, means that you are turning your inventory over that many times a year. In general, the more often you turn your inventory over the better off you are. But once again, each industry has its own norms. A business in a very changeable industry (fashion, for example) may have to turn inventory over six times a year, while one in a static industry (home appliances, for example) may only need to turn over its inventory twice a year.

Most accountants would be content to draft a monthly or quarterly income statement, pronounce you solvent, and leave it at that. Unfortunately, many entrepreneurs—particularly retailers—go along with this. Some retailers I have interviewed and counseled had no idea of their cash flow. They couldn't tell me how many times their inventory turned over. They had no idea how much profit they made, if any, on every dollar in sales. They simply saw that they were making sales and paying their bills, and assumed that meant they were in good shape. In many cases they were, but only because they had deep pockets they could dip into when the business was short of cash or because they had an instinctive understanding of inventory.

Some entrepreneurs will become successful solely on instinct. But to *insure* that you will be successful you will have to take control of the situation and become an active observer of, as well as a participant in, the business. Keep on top of your cash flow. Understand your assumptions. Check your ratios constantly. Work at keeping your buying terms and credit policy advantageous. Routinely figure out your profit percentages.

Accountants—if they are selected wisely when entrepreneurs' teams are assembled—will be able to do more than just draft monthly or quarterly financial statements. They'll draw up cash flow statements and set up a cash budget that gives you the insight you need into your business's health. They'll institute a bookkeeping system that will let you check your ratios regularly. And most of all, they'll teach you the basics of business finance.

But accountants can only present you with facts and put them in context. They're like newspaper reporters. You, the entrepreneur, must be the editor-in-chief. Your responsibility is to make judgments and decisions based on the facts given you. Don't despair though, because along with the responsibilities come the rewards.

CHAPTER FIFTEEN

How to Pick a Partner

Each player on this team—
whether he shines in the spotlight
of the backfield or eats dirt in the line
—must be an All-American.
—OMAR BRADLEY

If you are thinking of going into business with a partner—
think again. Two heads aren't necessarily better than one.
Partnership opens up a whole new set of potential problems
for entrepreneurs who already are faced with a daunting task.
Partnerships should never be entered into casually. You may
have a good friend who shares your enthusiasm for freedom
from employment, but that doesn't mean he or she should
become your partner. Entrepreneurship may be lonely, but
that doesn't justify forming a partnership. You'll probably be
so busy that you won't have time to be lonely.

The only individual who automatically qualifies for partnership in your venture is your spouse—and that need not be
a formal partnership. Make sure there is a sound business
reason for taking on a partner. Actually, there are only two
good reasons for taking on a partner or partners: money and
management.

Taking on a partner immediately doubles your sources of
capital—or at least it should. A partner will have his or her
own money as well as family and friends to approach for
investments. That may be reason enough to take on a partner. Many successful businesses have been launched by
partners—one having the idea and the skill to carry it out, the
other having the money. If money is all you're after, try to
offer your partner as limited a role in the management of the
business as possible.

Perhaps you don't have the total package of traits and
skills you'll need to start and operate a successful business.
You can augment your mosaic with that of a partner. Let's say
that you have all the entrepreneurial traits but are lacking in
management skills, or that you have the entrepreneurial traits
and management skills but have no experience in the business you are entering. It's possible to compensate for your
deficiencies by taking on a partner who has just the skills,
traits, or experience you lack.

I know of two such entrepreneurs who became partners in
a financial consulting business. Their partnership was extraordinary. Not only did they combine their traits to form a
solid entrepreneurial package, but their lives and personalities, at least in the office, began to become intertwined. Their
desks were in the same room, facing each other. Invariably

they would both get on the telephone, or both take part in a meeting—sometimes even finishing each other's sentences. Their relationship was so symbiotic that they were always referred to as a unit, never individually.

Sometimes, however, a partner's traits can be a double-edged sword. I've picked partners who were shrewd and cunning, ruthless in their negotiations. Unfortunately, these traits—which I thought were assets to our business—were occasionally turned on me. A partner's personality may also change over the years. He or she can become a gambler or start to drink or take drugs to excess. The daring and brave individual you started the business with can become stodgy and conservative over time.

Partnerships only work if they complete an otherwise incomplete equation—and if they are more than the sum of their parts. Entrepreneurs who are already complete—in talent, capital, and so forth—can only do themselves and the business harm by taking on partners.

This can be especially harmful when family members become partners. A very successful small business person I know decided to bring his son into the business as a partner. Rather than having the son begin as an employee and then take over ownership once the father retired, the two men thought they could run things together. It was a nightmare. After one year, the two partners—father and son—stopped speaking to each other. If the name of one was mentioned to the other the response was a string of insults and epithets. The business was eventually sold, and with its dissolution the relationship between the two revived. The family survived their partnership—but the business didn't.

Remember that when you take on partners you become accountable to them. Each partner is an agent of the business. A partner can bind you to an agreement without your knowledge, perhaps jeopardizing the business. Third parties can sue you for your partner's actions. That's why it is essential to thoroughly interview and investigate any potential partner.

There can be no secrets between business partners. The personal liabilities of partners cannot be held against a business, but it is possible that your partner's creditor could suddenly become your new partner.

It's possible to take on a partner at any time during the evolution of the business. Unbundling, and all its problems, can be avoided by taking on a partner who can assume some of the responsibilities you're being forced to delegate. Likewise, when second-tier financing is vital, a partner may be brought on board, eliminating the need to go after venture capitalists or bankers.

Whatever your reason is for taking on a partner, your personalities had better mesh. You don't want a partner who has different feelings about working than you do. Your goals can't be too divergent. If your partner is looking to make money, and you are looking to grow a business, there are bound to be problems ahead. While the two (or more) partners need not be clones, they should have similar ideas and philosophies.

Silent partners are often the best partners—as long as they remain silent. When the business is progressing according to plan, silent partners will often stay contentedly in the shadows. But if problems crop up you could suddenly find your silent partner looking to play a more active role in the management of the business. Partners who once were content to do their half of the work may suddenly want to change jobs if the business gets into trouble.

Partnerships can be more involving than marriages. Marriage problems can drag you down emotionally. Business partnership problems can drag you down emotionally *and* financially. For that and other reasons, it is essential to have a legally constructed agreement that spells out the rights and responsibilities of all parties.

Your attorney should draw up a partnership agreement that puts in writing all aspects of the relationship between the partners. If you don't have your own partnership agreement, your business will fall under the Uniform Partnership Law (UPL), a piece of well-meaning but inadequate legislation that has been adopted by most states.

The UPL shouldn't be relied upon, as it makes some sweeping generalizations that can be extremely detrimental to the long-term health of a business. First, it states that each partner is entitled to an equal share in the profits. It also states that each partner has an equal share in the management of the business. Under the UPL, partners are obligated to contribute equally toward losses, work for their share in the business profits, and submit to a majority vote or arbitration. In the event that one partner dies, under the provisions of the UPL, the partnership ceases to exist. It does not allow for an estate to take over partnership interests. The business must be liquidated.

To avoid these pitfalls, and to assure a smooth working relationship, a customized partnership agreement must be drawn up. It should address specific financial questions peculiar to the business: How much money will each partner be investing? When and how will they be paid back? Will there be any salaries drawn, and if so, how much? What share of the profit will each partner receive?

Nothing lasts forever, so your partnership agreement has to have written into it the means of dissolving the partnership. How and when can one partner buy out the other? Can partnership rights be passed on to estates, or do they immediately revert to the surviving partner? How are proceeds from the sale of the business to be divided among the partners?

If you are taking on a partner after the business has been operating for some time—perhaps as a way to unbundle— you'll also need a partnership agreement. This one, however, must contain an additional provision describing exactly which of the business's liabilities the new partner is responsible for. Common law usually limits new partner liability to only the money they invest in the business. In other words, your new partner cannot have his or her personal property attached by creditors. Make sure your agreement addresses this issue.

All potential problems must be addressed in the partnership agreement. Once the business's structure is clarified in a legally binding agreement, the partners can devote their energies to running the business, not worrying about each other.

You don't have to develop a personal relationship with a business partner. In fact, it can cause problems. Think twice before you socialize with your partner or his or her family. It is enough that you have to spend fourteen hours a day, maybe seven days a week with a partner.

I was once involved in a business partnership that turned into a social relationship. My wife and I would go out with my partner and his wife. Unfortunately, my partner's wife and I didn't get along. My problems with her cast a pall over my business relationship with her husband. Today, he is my former partner.

CHAPTER SIXTEEN

Buying an Existing Business

You do as chapmen do,
Depraise the thing you desire to buy.
—WILLIAM SHAKESPEARE

Starting a business from scratch may well be the truest form of entrepreneurship, yet it's also possible to go out on your own by buying an existing business. This option may not suit every individual with an entrepreneurial personality, however. The person who buys a business is more cautious, perhaps a little less creative, but no less an entrepreneur than the individual who starts his or her own business.

While it doesn't match the textbook definition of entrepreneurship, buying an existing business does have certain advantages. It is intrinsically less risky than starting a business from scratch. You'll realize profits quicker. You'll get a faster return on your initial investments of time and money. An existing business has a track record. All its financial and marketing plans have been put in action. It has a location, equipment, inventory, customer base, and staff. With one financial transaction you will be able to step into the owner's shoes. You won't have to dig into your own pocket or keep going back to investors if you have enough working capital.

That doesn't mean it is risk-free. All the potential positives could just as easy evolve into negatives. It is just as easy to inherit ill will as goodwill from the previous owner of the business. The current staff of the business may be incompetent or unmanageable. Facilities and equipment may need to be modernized. Inventory could well be obsolete. The location could be too expensive or inadequate for expansion. In order to avoid these pitfalls, entrepreneurs looking to buy an existing business will have to work just as hard as if they were starting their own business.

WHAT TYPE OF BUSINESS SHOULD YOU BUY?

The first step is to decide what type of business you want to buy. Examine your personality, skills, and experience. What type of business would you do best in? Forget about buying a business just because it's for sale, it's doing well, or the price is right.

Narrow your search to businesses with which you have experience and expertise. Unlike the entrepreneur who starts his or her own business, the person who buys an existing business will have to step right in as owner/operator—there is no time to learn on the job. Also, without experience in the particular business you won't be able to make an evaluation of a business for sale.

Remember that the seller is always selling for a reason. It is possible to hit gold and find a business owner who is really selling because of illness or impending retirement. Perhaps you can find a business whose owner died that is now being shopped around by an estate. But more than likely the business is up for sale because there is something wrong with it. These reasons, of course, will probably be well concealed. Remember, the seller is probably an entrepreneur also. He or she will know all the tricks of image and financial management that are outlined in this book. Unless you have enough experience to make an intelligent analysis, you can get taken to the cleaners.

In order to effectively analyze a business that's up for sale you will have to be objective. Don't let your dreams or a seller's camouflage blind you to reality. Fall in love with the business after you own it, not before. You will need to have enough financial acumen and objectivity to evaluate all the numbers and records of the business and to know what you could do to improve them. Finally, you should know enough about the industry to tell whether the business is worth purchasing.

SEARCHING FOR TARGETS

With the self-analysis behind you, start on the search for a business. Ask your professionals if they know of any business for sale. Accountants and attorneys may be privy to knowledge that could help your search. Speak to your own and other bankers about leads. Trade associations could also be helpful. Try canvassing auctioneers of distressed businesses. They'll keep on the lookout for a business for you, since it will be easy for them to sell all the assets to you. Consult the classified ads in major newspapers and trade journals.

Examine the business-for-sale ads carefully. The more details offered, the more serious the attempt to sell. If there is a phone number or address indicated you will probably be able to deal directly with the owner. Box numbers generally indicate an attempt to obscure something. More than likely, ads with box numbers will lead you to a business broker rather than an owner. But that may not be all bad.

Business brokers, like real estate brokers, earn commissions on the sale of a business. They collect their money only when a deal has been closed. Treat them exactly as you would a real estate broker. At best, business brokers represent the deal. At worst, they represent the seller's interest. While it isn't necessary to go through business brokers when looking for a business to buy, they can be helpful. They are sure to have more than one property up for sale, and may, in fact, have a host of potential businesses for you. Check their reputations by asking for references and talking to your professional team. A good business broker can speed up your search. There is a drawback to using them, however. Invariably, the deal negotiated through a broker will go for a higher price than one negotiated directly—if only to make up for the commission.

Good business opportunities don't grow on trees. If there is nothing for sale in your immediate area that fits your needs, try to make something for sale. Remember, every single business is always up for sale—whether or not the current owner knows it. Everyone has a price. Telling a business owner that you want to take care of him or her for the rest of his or her life is an attractive proposal—especially for another entrepreneur who has sweated and struggled for years to make a business work. Presenting the purchase of the business as a life-long income can make even the most contented business owner sit up and take notice.

If your attempts at forcing a business onto the market are fruitless you may have to move. You can't operate most businesses long distance. They will require hands-on management. Resolve that you will pick up stakes and relocate for the right business opportunity. If you can't bring yourself to move, you're not the right kind of person to buy an existing business. That doesn't mean you have no other alternatives— you can always start a business or buy a franchise.

ANALYZE YOUR PROSPECTS

Once you've found some leads, it is time to start analyzing the prospects. Begin your analysis with a complete study of the location. This should be just as thorough as if you were starting a business from scratch. Follow the guidelines I discussed in Chapter Six: Selecting Your Location. Are there new shopping centers opening nearby? What is the character of the area? Is there evidence of new construction? Is there sufficient parking? Are traffic routes and patterns favorable? What is the attitude of local government toward business? Once you're convinced that the location is viable start examining the nuts and bolts of the business.

The only way these can be uncovered is through a well-planned investigation—an investigation backed by a team of savvy professionals. This analysis is too complex for an individual to do alone. You will need the services of lawyers, accountants, and perhaps business appraisers, consultants, and bankers.

From the beginning the services of your lawyer and accountant will be indispensable. Enlist professionals who have experience negotiating the purchases of businesses and expertise in the particular business you are entering. Fees may add up, but their experience and expertise can save you from disaster. Their judgments may not be flawless, but their presence on your team will improve your odds dramatically. Their objectivity will be a good counterweight to your natural enthusiasm. Remember that lawyers will be absorbed with legal issues and accountants with financial issues. Get their efforts to mesh. Hold frequent meetings with both of them present.

Begin your investigation with some basic inquiries:

• How long has the business existed; who founded it; how many owners have there been?

A business that has existed in the same location for many years will have built up more goodwill than a new enterprise, or one that has just moved to its present location. A high turnover in ownership can only mean trouble. Founders are tougher to deal with than either operators or heirs—original entrepreneurs will look on the sale of their business as an emotional as well as a financial transaction. After all, the business is their "baby."

- Is the business profitable? Are profits increasing or decreasing? Why? How can I improve it?

You'll need to look at the financial records for at least the past five years. In order to get this all of this information you will need to get a wide range of documents including balance sheets, income statements, tax returns—both federal and local—and other financial statements all prepared by a CPA and put into comparative form for easy analysis. Have your accountant go over the financial statements and put your attorney to work performing a lien and judgment search on the owners and the hard assets of the business. Check with Dun & Bradstreet for additional financial background information.

While important, tax returns aren't sufficient evidence of the profitability of a business. A sizable percentage of small businesses try to obscure some of their profit to avoid paying heavy taxes. But don't rely on figures on the back of a brown paper bag or from a "second set" of books. Study the operating expenses and try and compare them with those of comparable, efficiently run businesses. You can find these by consulting trade associations, which often keep abreast of industry averages. Get records of bank deposits. Check the bills paid to suppliers and reconcile them with sales records. Profits may also be overstated. Is there evidence of a hesitancy to write off bad debts? Are fixed assets, such as equipment, under-depreciated? Is inventory overstated?

Your accountant has to try to "purify" the company's income statements. All the personal expenses of the previous owner—salary, perquisites, travel, and entertainment—have to be removed from the financial statements. Once this is accomplished, all of your own personal expenses have to be factored in.

Profit has to be analyzed with an eye on the investment you'd be making in the business and the projected future sales volume. Work up the ratios of the business and compare them to industry averages, again obtainable from trade associations. Is the rent too high a percentage of operating costs?

Are salaries out of line with sales volume? Is inventory too large? Are advertising costs too high or too low? Run the same ratio tests a lender would. (See Chapter Eleven: Second-Tier Financing and Chapter Fourteen: Financial Management.) Figure out what you as the new owner could do to improve these ratios, but keep it to yourself.

· Scrutinize the nature of the tangible assets you'd be buying.

What is the condition of the inventory? Is it fresh or obsolete? Check how quickly inventory turns over. Is the inventory saleable? Is there a good range of sizes, styles and colors? Does the inventory mix match the local market?

Take a good look at equipment. Is it in good condition? Who owns it? Are there liens against any of it? How does it compare with competitors' equipment? Technology changes quickly and many business owners fail to keep up. Ancient cash registers won't cut it today. Most businesses up for sale will suffer from obsolete equipment. Also be sure to check that the insurance coverage is in line with the value of assets.

· Study the intangible assets—goodwill—you'd be buying.

Contact independent business brokers, appraisers, or consultants to get a third-party view of the business's intangible value. Ask suppliers and trade associations about the reputation of the business. Is there really goodwill, or has the owner a reputation for poor service? "Under new management" signs will never make up for a bad reputation. Does the business hold any franchise, patent, copyright, or trademark rights? How valuable are they?

· Look at the business lease, licenses, and other contracts.

How long does the lease run? What are its conditions? Is it assignable? Can it be renewed? Are rent escalations spelled out? A business and its lease are inseparable. You can't buy goodwill if you are forced to relocate due to a poor lease. Does the business have any employment contracts expiring soon? Are licenses up for renewal?

• Study the sources of supply.

Are they adequate? Do they offer good service? Are the suppliers state-of-the-art or second-class? What are the reputations of suppliers? Are any franchise or special arrangements due to expire in the near future? Are contracts falling due? What is the likelihood of renegotiating or extending agreements?

• Study the competition.

How many competitors are there now, and how many are there likely to be in the future? How do they compare with the business you are thinking of buying? Are new methods or substitute products looming on the horizon? Competition is healthy when markets aren't local. Two competitive manufacturers in close proximity can team up and improve each other's businesses. Retailers of shopping goods—shoes, clothing, jewelry, or furniture—benefit from being near competitors. Consumers can make one trip to make their purchases. Retailers of staple goods—supermarkets, and so forth—suffer from nearby competition. Service businesses likewise are hurt by neighboring competitors.

• Study the personnel of the business.

Are the employees competent? Is there sufficient staff? Find out about the key individuals. Are they willing to remain after the ownership shifts? Does the owner have any special personal connections or relationships that are important for the continued health of the business? Are labor costs too high, dragging down profitability? Labor costs might also be too low, forcing a new owner into an immediate increase if he or she wishes to hold on to staff.

• Ascertain why the owner wants to sell.

Is the client base diminishing? Are there supply problems or employee problems? Maybe the plant and facilities are obsolete, there are disputes with the landlord, or creditors are after the seller. The business may be getting too big for the current owner—perhaps he or she is a pioneer who can't become a manager—in other words, an entrepreneur who can't unbundle.

Never take the seller's word for why they are selling. Sellers commonly hide the true reason and instead offer "good" reasons. Be skeptical about what you hear and try to dig deep enough to find the true reason. What will they do after selling the business? Where will they go?

Speak to customers, suppliers, the local banker, and other merchants. Never feel timid about seeking information. Anything goes in this type of investigation. If you ever feel hesitant, just remember that the seller will be doing everything in his or her power to inflate the value of the business and obscure its problems.

In most cases, fear underlies the desire to sell a business: fear about the financial future; fear that wealth built up in the business will soon be lost; fear that new technology is beyond the entrepreneur's scope; fear that their products or services are outdated. There are valid reasons to sell a business— almost all are personal and career-oriented. Owners may wish to convert their holding to cash and retire. There may be questions about management succession—perhaps a problem with heirs. Poor health may be the problem.

The true motivation for selling is probably a combination of factors. In any case, try to get to the truth. If poor health is cited, speak to the physicians involved. Probe every answer. Leave no stone unturned. Knowing the true reason for selling will be invaluable ammunition when negotiating the price.

DECIDING ON A PURCHASE STRATEGY

There are two ways to buy a business: purchase the balance sheet or purchase the assets. Purchasing a balance sheet means taking over both the assets and the liabilities of the business. Most sellers prefer this technique. Buyers, however, will do better simply by purchasing the assets and letting the previous owner dissolve the company and take care of any liabilities. That way you don't have to live with the seller's history. Prior tax returns of the business might be subject to audit. Lawsuits might arise from actions taken in the past. If you make a bulk purchase of the assets you cannot be held liable for actions of the previous owner.

SETTING THE PRICE

The next step is to decide how much the business is worth. The purchase price of a business has to depend on the ability of the business to make a profit for you. It must be a better investment than other, more traditional investments, and compare favorably with starting a new business.

There are four ways to determine the value of a business: by liquidation value, by book value, by market value, and by formula value.

The **liquidation value** of a business is arrived at by calculating what the tangible assets of the business would bring at auction. Accounts receivable are reduced to a safe value. Equipment is priced at the second-hand level. Inventory is treated as if priced for a distressed sale. It is the lowest value you can assign to a business, and the most desirable way to buy. But since most of the businesses you'll be looking at are going concerns, it isn't realistic to assume you'll be able to pay just the liquidation value.

The **book value** of a business is simply the value listed in the books of the business. Every asset's value is set at cost minus depreciation. You assign full value to inventory, without correcting for obsolescence. This is an easy way to make a rough estimate of what it would cost you to buy a business.

A better way to estimate price is to look at the **market value** of a business, which reflects an accepted expert estimate—often made by a business broker or accountant. It is based on rules of thumb acquired through years of experience. Its usefulness is in ascertaining the general price range for a business you are interested in.

Certified public accountant/attorney Stuart Rosenblum has made a nationwide study of the market values of various types of businesses. The chart on pages 210–12 was prepared for this book—and describes the formulas used to establish market value.

DETERMINING THE MARKET VALUE OF A BUSINESS

Business	Price Multiplier	Important Conditions	Watch for
Apparel Store	.75 to 1.5 times net plus equipment and inventory	Location, competition, reputation, specialization	Unfavorable shopping patterns, inadequate parking, outdated inventory
Beauty Shop	.25 to .75 times gross plus equipment and inventory	Location, reputation, boutique image	Excessive staff turnover
Bookkeeping Practice	.5 to 1 times gross plus equipment	Transferability of clients, client retention history, types of clients	Slow-paying clients, inadequate fee levels
Building Supply	.05 to .1 times gross plus equipment and inventory	Location, competition, lease terms, quality of inventory	Obsolete inventory, inadequate parking, chain store competition
Car Repair Shop	1 to 2 times net plus equipment and inventory	Reputation, referrals, condition of premises, location, lease terms	Lack of referrals or insurance company work, high- versus low-end repairs
Car Dealership	1.25 to 2 times net plus equipment	Type of dealership, reputation of company, location	Brand new manufacturers, factory allocation policy
Car Wash (Full Service)	1.25 to 1.75 times gross with equipment	Location, reputation, condition of equipment, lease terms	Distance from main arteries, worn-out equipment
Cocktail Lounge	.35 to .75 times gross with equipment and inventory	Transferability of liquor license, location, lease terms	History of license violations, inadequate volume

Notes:
1. Gross = gross income
2. Net = net income
3. Equipment and inventory = at fair market value

Business	Price Multiplier	Important Conditions	Watch for
Coin-Operated Business	.75 to 1.5 times gross with equipment	Location, condition of equipment, service types, lease terms	Poor visibility, income level of customers
CPA Practice	.75 to 1.5 times gross plus equipment and inventory	Types of clients, client retention history, ease of transfer	Aging or slow-paying clients, work quality
Dental Practice	.75 to 1.25 times net with equipment	Patient demographics, transferability of patients, lease terms	Lack of referrals, slow-paying patients, demographics resulting in too good dental hygiene
Distributor	1.5 to 2.5 times net with equipment	Market need for product, quality of manufacturer relations	Products in decline, slow-paying customers, lack of growth
Employment Agency	.75 to 1 times gross with equipment	Reputation, client relations, specialization	Excessive staff turnover
Fast Food Restaurant	1 to 1.25 times net	Location, competition, neatness of premises, lease terms	Inadequate street traffic, inadequate servicing space or seating area
Funeral Home	.75 to 1 times gross plus equipment	Reputation, quality of facilities, demographics	Number of funerals, community acceptance
Gas Station	$1.25 to $2.00 per gallon pumped per month with equipment	Gallons/month, location, competition, other services, lease terms	Poor traffic pattern, short lease
Grocery Store	.25 to .33 times gross with equipment	Location, lease terms, condition of facilities, presence of liquor	Nearby supermarkets or convenience stores
Insurance Office	1 to 2 times annual renewal commissions	Client demographics and transferability, carrier characteristics	Agent turnover, account mix

Business	Price Multiplier	Important Conditions	Watch for
Manufacturer	1.5 to 2.5 times net with equipment plus inventory	Distributor relations, market position for products, condition of plant	Single major customer, foreign competition
Newspaper	.75 to 1.25 times gross with equipment	Location, demographics, economic conditions, competition, lease terms	Stagnant or declining community
Telephone Answering Service	2.5 to 3.5 times net with equipment	Reputation, competition, employee turnover	Rude operators, high customer turnover
Real Estate Office	.75 to 1.5 times gross with equipment	Tenure of salespeople, franchised office, reputation	Intensity of competition
Restaurant	.25 to .5 times gross with equipment	Competition, location, reputation	Predecessor failures
Retail Business	.75 to 1.5 times net plus equipment and inventory	Location, competition, reputation, specialization, lease terms	Obsolete inventory, chain store competition
Travel Agency	.04 to .1 times gross with equipment	Revenue mix, location, reputation, lease terms	Negative climate for international travel
Video Shop	1 to 2 times net plus equipment	Location, competition, inventory	Obsolescence of tapes, match of tapes to customer base

Sellers are always adding premiums for goodwill. The best way to think of goodwill is as the payment you make to the original entrepreneur for all the mistakes and problems he or she had while growing the business to its present level. Unfortunately, you can't really quantify how much this is worth to you. In fact, determining the value of goodwill is the most difficult part of buying a business. It is most often calculated as how much more money you could make by investing in this particular business, rather than a comparable, more conventional investment. That's a complicated concept, but one that is essential to grasp if you're going to be able to set a price on an existing business.

The single best way to set a price on a business that includes fair valuation of goodwill is to determine the business's **formula value.**

The first step in this formula is to establish the adjusted value of the tangible assets. In other words, subtract total liabilities from total assets. Rather than using the numbers from the seller's balance sheet, make judgments based on the research you have done. Let's assume that you determine the adjusted value of the tangible assets to be $100,000.

Next, estimate how much you could earn annually by placing that amount ($100,000) in some other type of investment. For example: if you put $100,000 in a Certificate of Deposit for a year you would probably earn 10 percent interest or $10,000.

Now, add the potential earnings ($10,000) to your current salary. If you aren't currently drawing a salary, use the salary you plan to draw as owner of the business. Let's say your current job pays you $25,000. By adding the potential earnings of $10,000 to your current salary of $25,000 you come up with a total of $35,000.

Take a look at the average annual net earnings of the business for the past three to five years. Net earnings is the net profit the business made before the owner took out a salary. For example: In 1986 the business had annual net earnings of $40,000. In 1987 the figure was $42,000. In 1988 it went up again to $44,000. The average of these three numbers is $42,000.

Now, subtract the total of earnings power and current salary ($35,000) from the average annual net earnings of the business ($42,000). The resulting number ($7,000) is called the extra earnings power of the business.

Using this extra earnings power, we can determine the value of the intangible assets of the business—its goodwill— by multiplying this number by a "certainty" figure. We come up with this figure by looking at how unique and powerful the goodwill seems to be, how long it would take to bring a new business up to this business's performance, and how well established the business is.

The more certain it is that the business will continue in the manner it has, the higher a certainty figure you should choose. Work with a range from 1 to 5. A business that has been around for twenty years, is well known, and is consistently profitable would get a certainty figure of 5. A business started a year ago, which doesn't have much reputation or track record of profitability, would get a certainty figure of 1. With that in mind, let's return to our example.

The business we are valuing has been around for eight years. It is fairly well known and has achieved a moderate amount of goodwill. The profit record has been good for more than five years now. Let's assign them a certainty figure of 3. By multiplying the extra earnings power ($7,000) by our certainty figure (3) we determine that the value of the intangible assets, or goodwill, of the business is $21,000.

The final step in the formula is to add the adjusted tangible net worth ($100,000) to the value of intangibles ($21,000). The resulting total ($121,000) is the formula value of the business.

As you can see, determining the value of a business is a subjective science at best. So many variables and assumptions come into play that it is a very inexact process. The best solution to this subjectiveness is to be a tough negotiator and get as good a deal as you can.

NEGOTIATING THE DEAL

You should never pay cash for an existing business. You have to make so many estimates that it is only natural to require the seller to guarantee his or her claims to some extent. That can be done by taking back paper—in effect, giving you a mortgage on the business. Try to have any paper taken back by the seller partially subordinated to lines of credit from bankers or investors.

In fact, the terms of the purchase can be more important than the actual purchase price. Obviously, the longer the terms, the lower the interest, and the more subordinated the debt, the better off you are. Tell the seller that you would like to take care of him or her for the rest of his or her life by setting up an annuity or a steady income.

The financial arrangements you make with the seller are limited only by law and the creativity of you and your accountant. There are no hard and fast rules about financing the purchase of a business—creative financing is alive and well.

To reduce your cash outlay you might consider "thinning out" the assets of the business you propose to purchase. Separate any real estate ownership from the business ownership. Buy the business but not the property itself, and have the current owner offer you a lease with an option to buy. Likewise, try to lease the equipment and fixtures from the seller, rather than purchase them outright. The seller can also purchase all the accounts receivable owed the business. Finally, it is also possible to buy a controlling interest rather than the entire business. This will assure the seller of a continuing role in management decisions. Agree to buy the balance upon the seller's death. These can all be presented as sources of income for the seller above and beyond the actual purchase price.

Based on your financial analysis, what problems did you see in the operation? If the rent was too high, try to make the contract subject to getting a reduction in rent. Similarly, if labor costs are inflated, make the contract subject to a reduction in salaries based on renegotiation or layoffs of superfluous personnel.

Feel free to charge for favors to the seller. If relatives or specific employees must be kept on, exploit this in your price negotiations.

The motivation for selling the business can play a large part in your negotiating strategy. If the seller is under stress use that to your advantage. Businesses sold by an estate rather than an owner/operator are worth less. A sizable amount of the goodwill of a business is tied up in the person of the owner. Factor his or her absence into your price negotiations.

Sellers may have an inflated view of the value of their business. Often it represents their life's work—it's their Taj Mahal. Try to get third parties—such as their own accountant or attorney—to bring grandiose visions down to earth. You can even "seduce" such owners by presenting yourself as the perfect person to carry on their business. Show how much you love their business. Demonstrate the affection and devotion you will shower on it. Let them know that you are the right person to follow in their footsteps.

If you've found a discrepancy in the financial information, or if the gross revenues can't be proven by the books, it isn't necessary to walk away from the deal—you can simply take that into account and lower your offer. Or you can take out an "insurance policy" by having the seller take back paper for that part of the purchase price you are unsure of and accept less if the figures don't prove out.

Purchasing an existing business can be a quicker and safer path to entrepreneurial success than starting a business from scratch—but only if it is done with considerable skill, research, investigation, and savvy negotiation. It is possible to get a "steal," but it is also possible to be taken.

CHAPTER SEVENTEEN

Buying a Franchise

Never tell people how *to do things.*
Tell them what *to do and they will*
surprise you with their ingenuity.
—GEORGE SMITH PATTON

Franchising is a business structure in which one party, the franchisor, allows another party, the franchisee, to distribute a licensed product or service. The franchisor generally provides the franchisee with assistance in starting and operating the business, which may include site selection, help in designing the facility, financial assistance—either direct or indirect—advertising, marketing and management, and employee training.

Franchising is less risky than starting a business from scratch or buying an existing business. Much of the work has been done for you by the franchisor. In effect, a franchisee is buying a piece of the franchisor's company.

Combining the incentives of personal small business ownership with the management skills of big business, franchising is well on its way to becoming the dominant form of retailing in America. More than 10 percent of American businesses are franchises—and they account for over 30 percent of retail sales. Bankruptcies of franchisees are extremely rare. Franchisors will go to great lengths to avoid having one of their operations shut its doors—even if that means buying the franchise back from the operator.

If you are eager to operate a small business but don't have confidence in your own ideas, franchising may be for you. The business will have been tested; you'll be dealing with a known product or service that has gained acceptance; there will be a track record of financial and marketing success; you'll get expert help in merchandising, inventory, location selection, and accounting practices; and there will be a national, or at least regional, advertising program you can tap.

Franchising has become a reasonably ethical industry. Early in its history many franchise operations were, to say the least, shady. Today the industry is partly regulated by the federal government and has a self-policing trade association. Franchisors are required to file disclosure statements with the federal government, and some state governments. These statements contain a wealth of information, including the backgrounds of the franchisor's officers, the organization's financial footing, obligations placed on the franchisee, responsibilities of the franchisor, lawsuits filed against the franchisor, and the names and addresses of the company's other franchisees.

While all this may mean that the entrepreneur will have an easier time evaluating the operation, and perhaps even bringing it to the break-even point, it doesn't mean franchising is the best route for everyone.

Franchisors place severe restrictions on how one of their franchises can be run, even to the extent of limiting what may be sold and how it may be sold. In addition, buying a franchise may require the entrepreneur to have more up-front capital, since the franchise itself costs a sizable amount of money. The franchisee won't be able to go out and bargain or negotiate costs, since he or she will be limited to one supplier—the franchisor. The franchise agreement often gives the franchisor the right to cancel the agreement for ambiguous, sometimes petty reasons. And the agreement often runs up to five years, requiring a renewal and sometimes additional payments upon expiration.

Some entrepreneurial personalities may not be suited to operating a franchise. Franchisees are different from entrepreneurs who start their own or buy someone else's business—owners of franchises must be able to accept the restrictions placed on their creativity. Even if they think they have a better way of doing something, they can't try it if it violates the franchise agreement. They have to be conformists, rather than nonconformists—if the traditional entrepreneur is a general, the operator of a franchise is a sergeant.

Franchises are, technically, not part of an individual's estate. They generally cannot be passed on to the franchisee's heirs. Most franchisors require either that the business be sold back to the parent company, or that potential purchasers go through the entire application process required of the original owner. As a rule, franchisors only pay for the tangible assets of a franchise they buy back—goodwill is almost never factored into a purchase price.

The two biggest myths about franchising are that franchisees can get rich and can become independent. Neither is true. Much of the proceeds from the business must be poured back into the franchise to meet the quotas and requirements of the franchisor. And the franchisee is required to follow the franchisor's dictates to the letter, regardless of his or her individual desires or market. It has been said that franchisors want franchisees who are smart enough to operate the system, but not smart enough to improve on it.

If, after weighing the added financial requirements and restrictions on your creativity against the security, assistance, and experience offered by the franchisor, you feel franchising is an option you want to explore, begin to analyze individual franchises. While most franchisors offer substantial management and employee training programs, it can't hurt to have some experience in the industry you are entering. There are an incredible variety of franchise businesses available in almost every conceivable industry, and there are terms and conditions peculiar to each. Yet at the heart of every franchise is the franchise agreement.

Franchise agreements usually contain provisions on the fees for buying a franchise, royalties that may be due the franchisor, the franchisee's investment requirements, inventory and record-keeping requirements, promotional and management services offered by the franchisor, the territorial rights of the franchisee, the term of the agreement, conditions for canceling the agreement, and the sale of the franchise license.

Put together a team of professionals—including attorneys and accountants experienced with franchising—to pick through the agreement. Franchisors may be regulated, but that doesn't mean their agreements don't contain dangerous clauses hidden in the fine print. Have your professionals keep an eye out for any clauses in the agreement that may be illegal in your area. Make sure you have an exclusive territory and that it is large enough to support the business.

When I was a venture capitalist I was approached by a franchisee. He had purchased a regional franchise to distribute a well-known soft drink. I thought the deal would be great. The product was a major factor in its market segment. The franchisee, and I as his lender, could reap tremendous financial rewards—or so I believed. My hopes were shattered, however, when I read the franchise agreement. It had a term of only one year and required a fee for renewal. Basically, the franchisor gave up nothing. Sure, the franchisee would get a decent income, but he was, in effect, a slave of the franchisor.

While your confidence in the success of your franchise may be high, it is essential to look into what happens if the business doesn't succeed. When and how can the franchisor and franchisee terminate the agreement? Is the initiation fee simply returned to the franchisee, or will the franchisor pay the market value, including goodwill, of the business? This cuts both ways: if you do very well, the franchisor may want to buy you out and run the business on its own; if you don't run it up to the franchisor's standards, it may also buy you out. Try to insert a provision requiring independent arbitration of goodwill value in your franchise agreement. The franchisor's right to buy out a franchisee may be used as a sword against the business person. The only way you can find this out is to contact other franchise holders and learn from their experiences.

Pay close attention to the fees and costs of buying the franchise. Franchisors often fail to tell the whole story, simply offering information on the cost of using their name and way of doing business. Check into equipment costs, lease deposits, inventory costs, credit policies, staff salaries, and royalties. Work up a business plan, just as if you were starting your own business. Analyze your working capital needs and start-up costs and compare them to the franchisor's projections for sales volume. Are the franchisor's projections realistic? Draw up a worst-case scenario on your own and see how it would affect your finances.

Besides examining the franchise agreement itself, potential franchisees must do their own market research. Franchisors will show you their own market studies, but take them with a sizable grain of salt. Remember, they are in the business of selling franchises and are going to present information that makes them look like a good bet for the future.

Examine the franchise just as if you were starting your own business, asking the same questions and making the same judgments. What competition will you have? Your franchise may start as an original idea, but if it works you'll be sure to attract competitors. Recently, there was a trend toward health-oriented fast food franchises. It wasn't long before the major fast food franchises jumped in with their own salad bars.

Research the proposed location of your business the same way you would if the franchisor didn't exist. Is there sufficient parking? What is the character of the community? Is your geographical area growing or shrinking? Can it support your business, and competitors, into the future?

Isolate exactly what you are buying. Products have a certain life cycle. A hot prospect today might be obsolete tomorrow. Make sure that the market will last at least as long as your franchise agreement, otherwise your deal isn't worth the paper it is printed on.

Take a close look at the services offered by the franchisor. Does the franchisor provide sufficient advertising and marketing? Are in-store promotional materials supplied? Is the training program continuing or simply an introductory course? Does the franchisor have a handle on trends in the industry and react to them with new products or services?

With all this information in hand, search out financing as if you were starting your own business. Quite often, lenders are more comfortable dealing with franchise businesses, since they assume good management. Just make sure that your franchise agreement doesn't inhibit lenders. Investors will want to make sure that they can sell the franchise to recoup their investment.

A thorough analysis of the franchising agreement and independent market research are essential if you are going to truly take advantage of the positive aspects of franchising. Otherwise you are buying on blind faith—and that's never a good idea.

CHAPTER EIGHTEEN

Tactics for Retail Businesses

*To found a great empire for the sole purpose
of raising up a people of customers, may at first sight
appear a project fit only for a nation of shopkeepers. It
is, however, a project altogether unfit for a nation of
shopkeepers; but extremely fit for a nation whose
government is influenced by shopkeepers.*
—ADAM SMITH

It wasn't long ago that retailing was the "black sheep" of the business world. Business analysts used the word "shopkeeper" as if it were an insult. American entrepreneurs had a love affair with manufacturing and thought that retailing was for less intelligent or less savvy business people. How times have changed!

Today, large corporations are scurrying around the country trying to buy up retail outlets. Manufacturers are opening their own "outlet" retail stores, or setting up franchise businesses—all in an effort to get into the very business they once thought beneath them: retailing. They have finally realized that retailing has remained healthy through periods of inflation and recession, has constantly increased in size and scope, and has remained a reliable source of proprietor profits. While the profit from an individual retail outlet may not be tempting to a major corporation, the profit from a chain of retail outlets can make its board's collective mouth water.

As I mentioned earlier in this book, I've never met a millionaire retailer. Yet they all seem to send their children to the best colleges, drive luxury cars, live in fine homes, and invariably pick up the check at dinner. Retail is hard work and may never make you rich. But it is infinitely creative, tremendously satisfying, and an excellent source of financial security for entrepreneurs who thrive on hard work, enjoy dealing with the public, want and need control over most aspects of the business, are flexible enough to meet changing taste patterns, have expertise in a specific industry, and have a flair for salesmanship.

While almost all the advice I've given in the previous chapters applies to the operation of a retail business, there are some specific tactics entrepreneurs should add to their arsenal if they want to succeed in retail. The tips deal with areas particularly important to retailers: working capital requirements, inventory management and control, location, marketing, personnel, and attitude.

WORKING CAPITAL REQUIREMENTS

Retailers have more problem with working capital than other business people. Before retailers can make a profit, they must invest in goods to sell—an inventory. While they are purchasing an inventory, they also must pay all the other overhead costs of doing business—rent, utilities, and so forth. That means that retailers must spend a great deal of cash before they can expect to bring any sales, and subsequently profit, into the business. In addition, if retailers give credit to their customers, it's possible they'll have to wait some time after a sale to see the cash.

The first way to overcome this problem is to insure that your start-up cost projections are accurate. For most retail businesses, inventory turns over three times a year. If you project that your total sales for the year will be $300,000, you will need opening inventory that should account for $100,000 in sales. Assuming, let's say, an average markup of 50 percent, you will have to spend $50,000 on your opening-day inventory. Make sure that you start the business with enough operating capital to buy this inventory and pay your other overhead costs for four months. At that point you should have sold your inventory and be ready to restock, using the profit from your sales. If you are lucky enough to have more operating capital than you need, set it aside for contingency expenses.

The second way to avoid the cash squeeze is to set up a smart credit policy. In most retail settings, it should be sufficient if you accept major credit cards. Let Visa and Mastercard provide the credit. Unfortunately, if your plan depends on sales to other businesses, you'll have to set aside more money to make up for the period between the sale and the payment.

INVENTORY MANAGEMENT AND CONTROL

It is vital for retailers to remember that profits come through turning over their inventory. The more often you turn over inventory, the greater your profits will be. *Don't* over-buy. Inventory cannot sit gathering dust in a storeroom. That risks obsolescence and directly affects your profit. Consult industry associations for information on the standard turnover ratios for your business.

Buying well is really the key to successful retailing. Balanced stock is essential. You must have just enough of each item. That means stocking the right number of sizes, colors, and styles. Products that are "hot" or seasonal must be stocked in sufficient quantity to meet demand, but not to excess. A huge inventory of air conditioners won't sell well in December. The same goes for promotional or sale items. Keep in mind that you may also have to stock accessory items that don't carry as high a markup as your standard items. Accessories add to your store's image even though they may not directly affect your bottom line.

In the early stages of your business, much of your inventory decision making will be speculative. That's why a knowledge of the industry is vital. Know what other, similar stores order. Apply that information to what you know about your target customers and market niche.

Once you have managed one inventory turnover you'll be able to order more accurately in the future. But if you wait until the end of one selling season to do an inventory analysis, you'll be losing money. Remember, any investment made in inventory that goes unsold affects your bottom line adversely—you'll have less to spend on your next inventory. Your products may not age well. You must constantly analyze your inventory and sales. Compare your projections to actual sales. Are any particular items sold out? Are some items selling more slowly than expected? Are you developing a glut of one particular color, size, or style?

Keep track of your sales and inventory, noting how much money each item is bringing in, and what sub-categories of the item are selling best. For example: If you are selling handmade toys, note how much money the sale of your Noah's Ark set is bringing in. At the same time, note how many of the large, medium, and small sets are being sold. All this can be accomplished through paperwork and accurate sales records, but the best method is to get a computerized cash register that can tabulate sales and immediately subtract items from an inventory database.

In order to make sure that your inventory turns over you may have to alter your pricing policy or marketing strategy. Stay flexible. As soon as you discover items aren't selling take action. Advertise slow-moving products. Display them more prominently. Encourage your salespeople to push them, perhaps by offering an added commission. As a last resort, cut your price. When first pricing your products, try to give yourself enough markup to later mark things down—to move them out of inventory, cover operating expenses, and still make a profit. For a retailer, price can never be etched in stone.

Keep in mind that the earlier you cut your price, the better off you are. An early price reduction won't have to be as drastic as a later one. Even though you may cut into your profit, it's better to turn the items over as soon as possible. There is an old adage in retailing: the first loss is the best loss. Your prime mission is to move your inventory. If you do that, your profits will take care of themselves.

LOCATION AND MARKETING

Location is more important to retailers than to other business people. Sales take place only when a customer enters the location. That means traffic and exposure are vital. Poor location is the single largest factor in retail failure. But no matter how good your location is, unless you have a good lease you won't be able to take advantage of it. Commercial real estate specialists always quote an old saying: The lease is the business and the business is the lease. What they mean is that unless you can stay in the same location for a long period of time, it is impossible to build up goodwill and a steady clientele. Likewise, when it comes time to sell the business, goodwill can only be passed on if it is possible for the new owner to remain in the same location.

Inextricably linked to location is marketing. A high-traffic location means lower advertising costs and vice versa. Retailers often overlook the single best advertising outlet available to them—their storefront. A high-traffic location is meaningless unless a retailer does something that draws passersby into the store. Retailers with good locations should spend as much money on their signs and window displays as they do on their advertising.

Your display windows should be enticing. They should draw customers in. Display windows should show exciting merchandise, beautifully presented. If the display shows a variety of products, prices should be indicated. A "lifestyle" display—which presents a style, rather than a shopping list— need not have price tags. If no display windows are available, the interior of the store should be set up to give it maximum exposure to outside.

Pay attention to all the customer's senses—the overall ambiance of a store is extremely important. Lighting should be bright and warm. Keep it uniform throughout the store to avoid shadows and contrasts. Artificial light should be diffused so as to cause no glare. A store should not only look wonderful but also feel wonderful. Have fresh flowers. Use your air conditioner liberally. Keep humidity at a comfortable level.

Lay out your store intelligently. Place the products that sell fastest and are your most profitable in your best location. Keep impulse items separate from other products. Try to take advantage of those products you sell that are "necessities." Place them in an out-of-the-way location and have customers pass by impulse items to get there. Non-customer areas— employee restrooms, offices, and storage rooms—should be in your worst locations.

PERSONNEL

Retailers often have major personnel problems. Since business volume varies dramatically according to the time of day and the day of the week, staff size has to be flexible. That usually means part-timers have to be employed in order to keep salary costs manageable. Unfortunately, part-timers need more training. Yet they can serve as a good pool from which to draw future full-time employees.

One excellent way of rewarding personnel is to offer store bonuses based on the sale of items that either carry high markups or must be cleared from inventory quickly. Try extending discounts to employees on the purchase of store merchandise. Not only is this an excellent fringe benefit, but it encourages the employee to become familiar with the store's stock. Salespeople who use the store's own products are more effective.

Encourage your salespeople to develop their own relationships with customers. Have them wear name badges—they personalize selling and add another dimension of warmth.

My family has a tradition—the Pollan pearls. When each of my three daughters turned twenty-one I bought them a string of pearls. The first time I went to buy pearls I dealt with a charming saleswoman at a major jewelry and gift store. She was so pleasant and caring that the next time I came into the store for something else I searched her out. I've bought all three sets of Pollan pearls from her—she has become part of the tradition. Now, I don't buy anything at the store except from her. I even call ahead to make sure she is working that day.

ATTITUDE

Personal selling skills are essential for an entrepreneur to succeed at retailing. Not only do you have to love your merchandise, but you have to love your customers as well. This need not be a smothering, overbearing love. That will turn off more people than it will charm. Smile. Show people you care about them. Treat each customer as an individual. Satisfy his or her personal needs. Shower affection on your merchandise and it will be translated into more sales. Customers will love your merchandise if they sense that you do.

When I was a young man I worked the five-dollar tie counter at B. Altman's—a major department store. Each morning I would lay out my ties carefully, making sure that none were wrinkled. Every day I placed different ties on top of the piles. My manager taught me how to hold the ties up to customers' collars. I would wrap them around my finger in such a way that it duplicated a perfect Half Windsor knot—complete with the ripple in the center. They sold like the proverbial hotcakes.

Good retailers have eyes in the back of their head. They are aware of everything that is happening in the store. There may be five customers being waited on by five different salespeople, yet retailers can spot where there's a problem that needs attention. They are gregarious, but not intrusive. When a customer comes in with a wet umbrella, the retailer finds a place for it to dry out.

Good retailers never rest or relax while in the store. No matter how they feel they must be on stage performing—moving around, rearranging products, dusting, and cleaning—and making sure their staff does the same. An active selling staff tells customers that they'll receive good service.

Memory is the greatest tool a retailer can have. When customers come in and are greeted by name and asked how their most recent purchase is working out, they will become customers for life.

CHAPTER NINETEEN

Tactics for Service Businesses

*There never was a bad man
that had ability for good service.*
—JOHN STARK

The environment for starting service businesses has never been better. In today's mature economy, more disposable dollars are spent on services than on products. As discretionary income goes up, people are realizing that they can make their lives easier and more enjoyable by paying others to do routine tasks for them. Hundreds of service businesses have sprung up in response to this consumer need. And consumers have discovered that they'd rather spend their hard-earned dollars on experiences—such as classes, cultural events, and travel—than on material goods. A whole new class of service businesses has evolved to fulfill these new needs. And as more women enter the job force the services they traditionally performed are being performed by service businesses. But even with such a healthy environment there are stumbling blocks.

The first is the difference between selling services and selling products. Products can be seen, touched, weighed, smelled, and tasted—in other words, consumers can sense their value. It's also possible for consumers to compare products, judging which is better, which is more valuable. Products are standardized, while services are not. Each and every widget is the same. None of this holds true for services. The value placed on a service is perceived, not sensed. Many factors are involved.

Potential clients weigh their time and its value against the cost of a service. They base their judgment of the quality of a service on a series of superficial perceptions. How do the service providers look? What is their experience? How educated are they? Do they know anyone else who has used the service?

Because of this, there has to be a close relationship between the client and the service provider. You will have to bend and shape your service to fit each individual consumer's needs. Selling and marketing efforts must concentrate on the benefits of using the service, not on the service itself. Reputation and image are essential in selling services. Clients are really buying you, not the service. (Turn back to Chapter Seven and reread the material on how to cultivate a good image.) Service providers must be excellent at what they do, comfortable with selling themselves, good time managers, project-oriented, self-starters, and able to separate their ego from the business.

Since good word-of-mouth publicity is vital, your services must be of the highest quality. Clients are likely to remember even the slightest mistake and forget about the good service you provided. The provider of a service must be an expert—there's no way around it. If clients think they can do the service just as well, they won't pay you to do it.

Service providers don't have to worry about inventory, but they do need to be concerned with time. The inventory of a service business is the number of hours in a workweek. Service providers can only do so much in a day, which means they have to maximize their time. Time management, rather than inventory management, is essential. Don't accept too many clients too soon. Train your staff, if you have one, to do some of the tasks for clients. This will free you to work on more important tasks. One psychotherapist I know has limited his practice to group therapy, allowing him to bill multiple clients for each hour. If you find that you have more clients than you can comfortably service, raise your prices.

One excellent tactic for starting a service business is to work out of your home. By forgoing a separate office location, a service entrepreneur can both cut back on seed capital needs and trim working capital requirements. Rent payments—often the single largest monthly cost in metropolitan areas—can be eliminated entirely. Along with this saving comes a host of lifestyle advantages. Bankers and vendors won't look askance at such an arrangement. In some parts of the country there is even a cachet to home businesses.

A home location may even improve the business. I started my current financial advising business out of my home and operated it there until my coop board objected. At that point I moved my business to a condominium apartment. I set it up as if it were a home. It affords clients an anonymity some of them desire. Others draw comfort from the warm, caring environment. The location is less sterile, which fits my personal consulting style. I seem more accessible and understanding because of the homelike ambiance.

Every service business can be operated from a home. In most cases, the service provider can visit the client rather than the reverse. If client visits are required it's possible to meet at outside locations. Try joining a private club that has comfortable, intimate meeting rooms. Work out an arrangement with a local restaurant to reserve a regular, secluded table. The options are really limitless.

Perhaps nothing is more vexing for a service business than setting a pricing policy. Start, of course, with an estimate of your overhead, being sure to include continuing education, professional dues, and publications. Calculate how many billable hours—ones in which you can be providing service rather than doing administrative work—you have each day. Next, try to determine how valuable your service is to a client. Look at comparable services and see what others in your field are charging. Some entrepreneurs even send spies into competitive businesses to get inside information on fees. Remember that there is a certain cachet to a higher price. Clients will place a higher value on your service if you do likewise.

My son had two friends—twin brothers—who started a trash-hauling business on Martha's Vineyard in Massachusetts. There was no garbage collection in some of the outlying communities; residents had to bring their own trash to the dump. The business was started as a way to earn money during the summer. It grew dramatically. After a few years the brothers decided to leave the garbage business and go into other fields. When they went around to their customers to notify them that pickups would stop, they were shocked at the response. Most of the customers were upset that they would have to drop off their own garbage. Many said to the brothers, "You guys charged so little; I would have paid twice that amount if you asked it." The brothers never realized the perceived value of their service. To them, hauling garbage was menial work. To their customers, however, it was a vital service.

Actually, it's possible that your services will be better received if you charge a higher price. Clients are more apt to listen to you and follow your instructions if they are paying a premium for your service. Clients of dietitians who charge a high price are bound to lose more weight.

Clients may try to negotiate price with service providers, asking, "Can't you do any better?" Your response has to be "I can't—that's the price." Treat it as a fact. Stress that it has nothing to do with you or your desire to help, it simply reflects the factual value of your services. Backing down and lowering your price tells the client that your services aren't as valuable as originally stated. In addition, if a client gets you to lower your price, he or she will never be sure that another client hasn't bargained you down even further. Hold the line on your fee—it will pay off.

CHAPTER TWENTY

Tactics for Home Businesses

A man travels the world over
in search of what he wants
and returns home to find it.
—GEORGE MOORE

Approximately thirteen million Americans have discovered that not only is home where the heart is, but it also can be where the money is. Home-based entrepreneurs can cut back substantially on their seed and working capital needs—since they don't have to rent space. They can also improve their quality of life by creating an environment that encourages their creativity, achieving a better balance between family and career, being able to live anywhere within reach of a phone, and continuing to work regardless of their age or physical condition.

Of course, using your home as a place of business limits the kinds of businesses you can start. Traditional retail, wholesale, and manufacturing are out of the question due to legal restrictions on the use of residential property. This means that you can either launch a service business or come up with an innovative approach to one of the other types of businesses. For example, entrepreneurs have used "satellite" retail locations and mail-order catalogs to launch successful home-based wholesale and retail businesses.

To truly succeed as a home-based entrepreneur you will need to follow the same principles and precepts as any other entrepreneur. Just because your business is located in your home doesn't mean you can take shortcuts or be less professional. Developing a business plan is mandatory, as is setting up a careful system of financial management. You're starting a business, not a hobby, and it should be treated with the same serious care that any business deserves. Any "shortcuts" you take in starting a home business are likely to turn into a "shortcut" back into working for someone else.

The first major obstacle for a home-based entrepreneur is setting up and equipping an office. It is important to realize that you will not be able to set up a perfect home office. That would require extensive remodeling and construction, and therefore would eliminate the financial advantages of operating your business from the home. Any money spent on remodeling is a "sunk investment" that can never really be recouped.

That doesn't mean, however, that you should simply start working from your dining room or guest room. Try to find a space that measures at least twelve feet by twelve feet, has a door, and is outside the normal traffic flow of your family. It's a plus if it has good natural light and can be easily heated and cooled. Your home office should also be convenient to a bathroom, but far enough from the kitchen so that the refrigerator isn't a constant distraction.

Don't make the mistake of overspending on equipment, supplies, and furnishings in order to assuage your lingering feelings that a home business isn't really legitimate. There are three main rules to remember: purchase only as much as you need; place the highest value on durability; and, all other things being equal, buy the smaller product.

The single most important piece of equipment in a home office is the telephone. No one expects to get a busy signal when calling a place of business, so it is best to have at least two business lines. If you can't afford two lines, have call-waiting installed. Being able to make conference calls can also be a big timesaver; just make sure you will use it at least once a week. Call forwarding, on the other hand, is usually unnecessary.

When buying a telephone, opt for reliability rather than gimmickry. A hold button and speed dialing are useful, but speaker phones aren't necessary. If you will have clients or customers in your office on a regular basis, invest in a separate extension for their use so they don't have to sit at your desk to make a call. Avoid car telephones like the plague: They can make you a slave to the business.

Your second purchase should be a good telephone answering machine. Buy a two-line, voice-activated unit that allows you to vary the number of times the phone will ring before the machine answers the call. Make sure that your machine allows you to retrieve calls from a remote location—that way you can keep up with your calls even when you're out of the office.

If you are torn between buying a computer and a typewriter, choose the computer. The added capabilities will more than make up for the higher cost. Your choice of a computer system should be determined by software, *not* hardware. Search for the program or programs that best fits your needs and then buy hardware that can run the programs. Don't join the technological race—ease of use and reliability are more important than owning the latest thing in technology. Daisy-wheel printers turn out letter-quality copy but are noisy and slow. Dot matrix printers are a bit faster, and are good for graphics, but do not turn out business-quality letters. Your best bet is to get a laser printer. While they are expensive, they are also fast, quiet, and produce beautiful print. Laser printers print clearly and quickly enough that they'll also cut down on your printing and photocopying needs—offsetting their high price.

A facsimile machine has become a necessity today, but don't install a dedicated telephone line for it unless you use it several times every day. Instead of getting caught up in the search for a high-speed machine, buy one that has an automatic document feeder. Similarly, look for a unit that cuts pages automatically. Memory is only worthwhile if you regularly send messages across the country or overseas.

Photocopiers are expensive, temperamental, and cumbersome. Buy or lease one only if you spend more than one hour a week at the copy shop. Don't rely on your facsimile machine to make copies, however. The paper is too expensive and the resulting copies are of poor quality.

When furnishing a home office, make sure to choose your chair carefully. You will be spending six to ten hours a day sitting at your desk, so an old dining room chair just won't do. Your desk, on the other hand, need not be fancy—you just need enough space to do your work. Remember, no one will measure you by how much you spend on your equipment or office furniture. Don't buy a conference table and chairs unless you plan on holding conferences, and only get a specially-designed computer table if you spend more than five hours a day at the machine. Purchase only as many filing cabinets as you need. You can always store old files in a closet, garage, or attic.

Once office space has been set up, the second major problem facing most home-based entrepreneurs is their tax status. While most IRS rules and regulations are complicated, those regarding home business deductions are actually quite straightforward. To deduct expenses for the business use of your home, you must actually be engaged in a trade or business. The portion of your home that you deduct must be used both *exclusively* and *regularly* as either your principal place of business or as a regular meeting place.

You may deduct expenses that are either directly or indirectly related to business. Direct expenses are those that benefit only the business portion of the home, while indirect expenses are those that benefit both the business and personal areas of the home. (Expenses that benefit only the personal areas of the home may not be deducted.) In order to calculate what portion of any indirect expense you may deduct, simply divide it by the percentage of your home space you use exclusively and regularly for business. For example: If your office occupies 10 percent of your home, and your total rent is $1,000, then $100 of your rent is deductible. There is no limit on the amount of expenses you can deduct as long as your total expenses, including depreciation, are less than or equal to your gross income from the business.

The IRS doesn't mandate any particular record-keeping system. All it requires is that you have evidence that you actually used the claimed part of your home exclusively and regularly for business and that you actually spent the expenses you claimed.

In addition to setting up an office and understanding their tax responsibilities, home-based entrepreneurs have three other unique problems to overcome: their own attitude, the attitudes of family and friends, and the attitudes of clients and potential customers.

Home-based entrepreneurs have only themselves to rely on for disciplined work habits. This means that procrastination can become a problem. The cure is to establish cues and patterns for starting work and to stick to them. Begin work as soon as a certain program comes on the radio; or walk around the block, and on your return, get to work as if you were first entering the office that day. Similarly, act as if you were in an informal but public office—that means getting washed and dressed each and every morning. *No* successful home-based entrepreneur works in a bathrobe. Stick to business during the day and set up regular times for lunch and coffee breaks. Schedule yourself religiously—even noting your errands and tasks on your calendar. Return phone calls by the end of the day or first thing the next morning. Become an obsessive list-maker, and use your time as efficiently and productively as possible.

Try to keep your obsessiveness in check, however. Many home-based workers have a hard time leaving their office. If you love what you are doing and your desk is right in the next room, it's easy for twelve-hour days to turn into twenty-hour days, and for weekends to turn into workdays. Remember that one of the reasons you started a home business was for the less formal lifestyle. Unless your lifestyle of choice is *no* lifestyle, you'll want to make sure that you get away from your desk on a regular basis. To be truly productive you need rest and time away from work. Establish a regular quitting time and stick to it every day. Don't answer your telephone after business hours, and ignore your answering machine until the start of the following business day. No one expects a traditional business to be available around the clock. Why should you be any different?

It may seem heartless to think of family members and friends as potential problems—especially since one major reason for working at home is to be closer to them. Family and friends, however, often think that a home business is somehow less demanding than a "real" business—and can turn into major obstacles to your success. For example, your spouse may feel free to drop in to make small talk or call up just to say hello. Friends and neighbors may stop by to chat or to have lunch since you are "at home."

You can nip these distractions in the bud by establishing ground rules on day one. Ask your spouse and friends to treat you as if you were working in a formal office out of the home. If someone calls to chat just tell them that you are at work and will call them when you leave the office. Schedule friendly lunches the same way you would a business meeting.

Finally, don't be misled: A home business will not let you be a primary care-giver for your young children. You have a choice of devoting your time to your work or to your child—you can't do both. Most young children are just not capable of differentiating between home-time and work-time when both take place under the same roof. This means that, if possible, you will have to arrange for child care during work hours. Sit down with your children and explain when they can and cannot come into your office.

You'll come across the fifth major problem facing home-based entrepreneurs—the attitudes of clients and potential customers—when you start arranging business meetings. Regardless of how well-equipped or designed your home office is, the mere fact that it's in your home can lead clients and customers to think less of your business. Whenever possible, schedule meetings at the other party's place of business. If protocol calls for you to play host, hold the meeting at a private club, hotel, or restaurant. You can further disguise your home location by purchasing space at a private postal drop or by renting a post office box.

The best way to make your location a moot point is to be as professional as possible in all your dealings with clients. The image you portray to the outside world—whether through your clothing, your letterhead, or the message on your answering machine—should be solid and traditional.

If your attempts at camouflaging your location fail, and a condescending client asks why in the world you work from home, try one of these responses:

- My clients prefer the privacy and confidentiality that my location offers.
- My clients prefer the relaxed atmosphere and personalized service I can offer from my home.
- It's more expensive for me, but it lets me spend more time with my family.
- The ambiance helps me concentrate and be more creative.

CHAPTER TWENTY-ONE

The Secrets of Success

Seest thou a man diligent in his business?
He shall stand before kings.
—THE BIBLE, PROVERBS

There are no shortcuts to starting and making a success of your own business. It's a long, demanding process requiring dedication, concentration, perseverance, and lots of hard work. In this book I've taken you step by step through the process, explaining how it's done and pointing out potential hazards. Throughout I've offered tips and pointers to help smooth your way. Most of these are based on the belief that there is a wealth of untapped strength within each of us. This philosophy is based on some fundamental and wonderfully simple principles that I've evolved in my thirty-five years of lending to and advising entrepreneurs—and being an entrepreneur. I'd like to share my "secrets of success" with you.

TRADITIONAL VALUES PAY OFF

One of the most exciting discoveries I ever made was that tradition works! When I was a younger man I scoffed at tradition. I thought it was old-fashioned thinking and therefore outdated. I was wrong. Traditionalism, in all its forms, pays off. The old ideas are still around because they continue to work. Through economic booms and busts, in war and peace, the traditional values work—and they continue to work today.

Many people think that to be a success in business you have to be tough and unethical. Movies, television, and books abound with portraits of the cunning corporate raider and the shifty operator. The stereotype is dead wrong. In fact, if you take on these traits I guarantee your business will fail.

The Ten Commandments, the Golden Rule, and all those values that our parents taught us are essential ingredients of a successful business. Care for your staff, your customers or clients—and even your suppliers and landlord. Treat others as you'd like to be treated. Work hard and give 110 percent effort at everything you do. Take care of your health. Pay attention to your physical appearance—you are selling yourself before your product or service. Smile. Offer help to those who need it. Treat everyone as a special individual. Be honest. Soak up knowledge like a sponge. People will respond.

LOOK FORWARD TO THE FUTURE

To succeed in business you have to feel positive about the future. You have to have hope that good things lie ahead. Some people wake up every morning with dread. They see only the difficulties ahead of them. If they could they would just pull the blanket over their heads and go back to sleep—forever. To be a successful entrepreneur, you have to wake up enthusiastic. Problems are just obstacles to overcome on the way to achieving your goals—and you *must* have goals. Look forward to the future. Learn from the past. But keep all your energies focused on the present.

EXPERIENCE IS VITAL

The first kind of experience you'll need to be successful is a general understanding of business—the relationship between buyer and seller in a capitalist society. I'm a reasonably good businessman. I've been a venture capitalist and a banker. I've been president of a public company. I've been a lecturer and business professor. Today, I'm a practicing attorney and financial advisor. Yet the experience I draw upon most in life I got working at the drug store in the Barbizon Hotel for Women in New York City.

Beginning as a stock boy at the age of fifteen, I worked my way up to soda dispenser, then sandwich man, and finally to the exalted position of sales clerk, which I held while attending law school. I learned to sweep the floor every hour. I learned to open every display case and dust each item daily. I learned to rearrange the impulse items near the cash register every day. I learned to treat customers with respect, care, and love. I learned business.

If you've read this far it should be clear to you that experience in the business you're entering is also essential. How can you know what will work unless you have firsthand knowledge of your industry? How can you work out marketing plans when you have no idea what has or hasn't worked for others? How can you buy and stock a healthy inventory without first seeing how others have done it?

Even if you have experience, that doesn't mean you should stop learning. A continuing professional education is vital. Join trade or professional associations. Attend conferences and seminars. Take an active role in the local Chamber of Commerce. Stay on top of trends in your industry and in your region.

Watch your competition like the morning news. Study what they are doing. If they have discovered a great new idea steal it, or come up with a better one. There is nothing un-American about emulating success.

BRING THE CUSTOMER TO YOU

You can have the most wonderful location, sell the most marvelous product, or provide the most astute service in the world—and still fail if you don't bring customers or clients to your business. Don't think that people will beat a path to your door just because you've opened. Sure, some will. But not enough for you to be successful. Get out there and bring them to your business.

Promote yourself tirelessly. Use every technique at your disposal. Keep in touch with the media. Stay attuned to possible public relations opportunities. Make speeches. If advertising is your best promotional method, refine your message constantly. Do whatever it takes to attract customers. Put a sandwich sign on and walk up and down the block if you have to—but bring them in to your business. And never think that you have enough customers or clients. Keep on seeking more.

START EARLY AND STOP LATE

I'm always amazed when I see businesses that open late, close for lunch, shut the doors early, or close for vacations. They are doomed to fail. One of the secrets of success is understanding that the more time you spend on the business, the more successful you'll be. Remember, you pay rent for twenty-four hours a day. Why not use most of them for business?

Similarly, you have to keep on working on your business every hour of the day. Don't stop and don't rest. All work and no play won't make you dull. The only time you should stop thinking about the business is when you are asleep—and then you should dream about it. Eat, breathe, and sleep business. You won't mind it if you love what you're doing—in fact, it will be fun.

LOVE WHAT YOU ARE DOING

Since you are making a 110 percent commitment to your business you had better love what you are doing. If you don't enjoy your business you'll never put the necessary effort into it. The mere fact of starting your own business should be enough to make you love it. If you buy an existing business or a franchise—you'll learn to love it. The business may not be your spouse, but it is one of your children. Treat it that way.

RESPECT YOUR EMPLOYEES

A happy place of business works well. Customers love coming into an operation where the employees are content; where they obviously love what they are doing. Treat your staff well. Make them feel like they are participants. Give your employees the opportunity to create victories. Say "we" instead of "I." No one objects to structure, as long as it is fair and based on respect. Any problems in the employee environment you've created will be noticed by customers.

YOU CAN'T DO IT ALONE

Regardless of how many skills you have, how determined you are, how much experience you have, or how hard you work, you can't succeed alone. No man is an island. Reach out to others for help and advice. That is a sign of intelligence and humility, not stupidity or weakness. You need your teammates—professionals, investors, lenders, vendors, and suppliers—to work in harmony. Take them as much into your confidence as you can. Treat friends and family as valued team members as well. Ask their advice and listen to what they have to say. Keep the lines of communication open. They can help you immeasurably.

TAKE CHARGE AND BE DECISIVE—IF IN DOUBT, DO IT

Your team can only offer advice and guidance. The final decision is always yours—that's what makes you the entrepreneur. Don't hesitate or procrastinate—both are deadly. While you are worrying over a decision—staring into the abyss troubled about what might happen—others are taking action, beating you to the punch. Each time you fail to do something you've missed an opportunity to become more successful. Nothing ever happens by itself in America.

Be pro-active, not reactive. Make things happen, don't wait for them to happen to you. No mistake is so large that it can't be corrected. Treat problems as obstacles—hurdles in your path to success. Don't try to run around obstacles, confront them head on.

HAVE A SET OF POLICIES

A policy is a description of how the business handles certain situations. For example: In every dispute is the customer always right? Will we always accept merchandise returned, whatever the reason? Your business should have a policy for every important set of circumstances. As new situations arise, create new policies to address them.

These policies, in the early stages of the business, help to define exactly how and why you do certain things. They are closely linked to the image you wish to project to the outside world. At some point the business will begin to take on a life of its own. Policies then serve as the brain for this independent life. They allow you, the entrepreneur, to instill your beliefs and values into the business.

SIGNAL GOOD MANAGEMENT

Investors and lenders stress that good management is the key factor in deciding whether to jump into a business with you. Yet none of them will ever define what they mean by good management. They stammer and stumble, muttering words like experience and knowledge. Actually, they are watching you, studying your actions and statements, trying to read whether you're a good manager. So you must send them the right signals.

The best way to signal your management skills is to show that you know your business cold. Know your numbers, and your industry, inside out. Let your knowledge speak for you. Study so hard that the information becomes ingrained on your brain. You'll never have to demonstrate knowledge—it will come on its own.

THE POWER OF SILENCE

If you don't know the answer to a question say so—and offer to find out. If you have nothing to say—say nothing.

THE SHORTCUT TO TRUST

When working with investors, professionals, suppliers, and customers, entrepreneurs must show that they can be trusted. Meetings generally are too short to actually demonstrate trustworthiness, and asking someone to trust you often results in just the opposite. Instead, take the shortcut to trust—show the other party you care about him or her.

GET OUT OF YOUR OWN WAY

Most of the obstacles we face, in life as well as in business, are of our own creation. We do things to ourselves we would never let others do to us. Those of who have an entrepreneurial streak tend to be extremely self-centered. We think that everything revolves around us. We believe that we alone can manage our world. This kind of attitude breeds problems.

Try to stop worrying about the repercussions of every action you take. Get out of your own way. If you are worried, or if you are depressed, start working. Take action. You'll find that when you are busy you aren't worried and you aren't depressed.

Stop trying to steer and row the boat of life at the same time. Concentrate on the rowing and let Fate do the steering.

You'll be amazed at how well things will turn out. We need goals, and we need strategies to reach those goals—but that's as far as we should go in writing our life script.

ACT AS IF EVERY DAY WERE OPENING DAY

Work at constantly re-inventing your business. Begin each day as if it were your opening day. Your business has to be a fresh flower in full bloom, not a drooping shadow of yesterday's brilliance. The world around you changes every day. To keep pace, your business should as well. At the end of every day ask yourself, "What business am I in?"

Your competition is out there, just waiting for you to sit back and rest on your laurels. Never stop thinking up new ideas, looking for original approaches, or formulating new directions. As soon as you begin to stagnate, your competitors will take advantage of you. They'll offer the freshness and originality you've lost. All businesses are heading either toward success or toward failure—there is no middle ground. The answer to that daily question should be ever-changing, ever-evolving. If you find yourself giving the same answer for months at a time, start looking around—there are bound to be competitors gathering like vultures.

The best way to keep your business fresh is to look at it not as a means to an end, but as an end in itself. You aren't in business to become famous, rich, or powerful. The goal is to start and grow a business. If that isn't enough—you're not an entrepreneur.

Don't worry—if you approach your business this way wealth is a sure by-product.

INDEX

ABOUT THE AUTHOR

Stephen Pollan, a nationally known financial consultant, has been seen on "Good Morning America" and "Today," and is the coauthor of *The Field Guide to Home Buying in America*, also with Mark Levine. Stephen Pollan lives in New York City and Mark Levine lives in Long Beach, New York.

3110